Geography and Trade

Gaston Eyskens
Lecture Series

Dollars, Debts, and Deficits
Rudiger Dornbusch, 1986

Geography and Trade
Paul Krugman, 1991

Geography and Trade

Paul Krugman

Published jointly by
Leuven University Press
Leuven, Belgium
and
The MIT Press
Cambridge, Massachusetts
London, England

Ordering Information:

Belgium, The Netherlands, and Luxembourg:
All orders should be addressed to Leuven University Press, Krakenstraat 3, B-3000, Leuven, Belgium.

United Kingdom, United States, and all areas outside of Continental Europe:
All orders should be addressed to MIT Press or its local distributor.

Continental Europe outside Belgium, The Netherlands, and Luxembourg:
All orders should be addressed either to MIT Press, London, or to Leuven University Press.

First MIT Press paperback edition, 1993

This book was set in Palatino by The MIT Press and printed and bound in the United States of America.

Library of Congress Cataloging-in-Publication Data

Krugman, Paul R.
    Geography and trade / Paul Krugman.
        p. cm.—(Gaston Eyskens lecture series)
    Includes bibliographical references and index.
    ISBN 0-262-11159-4 (HB), 0-262-61086-8 (PB)
        1. Commercial geography—Mathematical models.
    2. Economic geography—Mathematical models.   3. Regional economic disparities—Mathematical models.   4. Industrial productivity—United States—Regional disparities—Mathematical models.
    I. Title.   II. Series.
    HF1025.K75   1991
    338.6'042—dc20   91-11984
                                                                      CIP

Contents

Foreword

The "Professor Dr. Gaston Eyskens Lectures" are published under the auspices of the chair established on the occasion of the promotion of Professor Doctor Gaston Eyskens to Professor Emeritus on 4 October 1975 and named after him. This chair is intended to promote the teaching of theoretical and applied economics by organizing biannually a series of lectures to be given by outstanding scholars.

The pursuance of this goal is made possible through an endowment fund established by numerous Belgian institutions and associations as an expression of their great appreciation for the long and fruitful teaching career of Professor Gaston Eyskens.

Born on 1 April 1905, Gaston Eyskens has taught at the Catholic University of Leuven since 1931. For an unusually large number of student generations Professor Eyskens has been the inspiring teacher of general economics, public finance, and macroeconomic theory. He is recognized as the founder of Dutch language economic education in Leuven. It should also be mentioned that he was a founder of the Center for Economic Studies of the Department of Economics. As a member of the governing board of the university from 1954 to 1968, he succeeded in adding an important dimension to the social service task of the university.

As member of parliament, minister, and head of government, he dominated the Belgian political scene for many years. His influence on the cultural and economic emancipation of the Flemish community has been enormous.

Professor Dr. M. Loeys

Chairman of the Administrative Committee of the Gaston Eyskens Chair

Preface

In October 1990 I had the honor and pleasure of giving the Gaston Eyskens lectures at the Catholic University of Leuven, in Belgium. This book consists of those three lectures, together with some supporting appendixes.

Putting together this kind of book is a rare privilege for the author, offering as it does exceptional scope for self-indulgence. One need not present ideas with the kind of buttoned-down rigor that is now mandatory in economics journals, nor need one display the sustained scholarly effort that justifies a monograph. Instead one is free to be loose, speculative, and occasionally silly. I am serious about the ideas presented here, but I was also having some fun with the presentation; I hope that readers will not take offense.

When Paul De Grauwe initially called me with the invitation to give the Eyskens lectures, we agreed that they would focus on the general issue of international factor mobility. It was clear that increased mobility of capital was a striking feature of the 1980s and that increased mobility of all factors would be a

likely consequence of increased European integration. I thought
that some interesting things about that increase in factor
mobility might be said from my own perspective on international trade, which emphasizes the role of increasing returns
and imperfect competition.

As I worked on the subject, however, I found that my analysis
was drifting further and further away from international
economics as I knew it. In international economics we take as
our base case a world in which resources are completely
immobile but in which goods can be costlessly traded. We may
then modify the model to introduce transport costs or nontraded goods, on one side, or mobile factors, on the other, but
the modeling style is clearly determined by the base case. And
as anyone who has done economic theory knows, the style of
our models strongly determines their content—issues that are
awkward to address are generally speaking not addressed.

What I found myself gravitating toward was a style of model
in which factors of production were perfectly mobile but in
which there were costs to transporting goods. In other words
I found myself doing something closer to classical location
theory than to international trade theory.

I could have entitled this book *Location and Trade*. I was afraid,
however, that this would convey too narrow an idea of what
I was trying to say. Although the intellectual tradition of
location theory is both wide and deep, what is taught is usually
a very narrow set of geometric tricks involving triangles and
hexagons. What I was after was not geometry but the fascinat-

ing issues that arise when firms must make interdependent spatial decisions. "Location" seemed too restrictive a term for this field. Location theory, however, is part of a much broader field, that of economic geography. Thus I have chosen to appropriate the term "geography" to describe what I am up to. I suspect that geographers proper will not be entirely pleased at what they see and may deny that the kind of stylized models that economists find appealing are part of their field. Nonetheless, I like the term and have appropriated it.

I argue in the lectures that the subject of economic geography is important in itself; it sheds considerable light on international economics, and it is a valuable laboratory for understanding economics in general. It is also fun. I had a very good time giving these lectures, and I hope that the readers of this book will have a good time too.

Geography and Trade

1   Center and Periphery

About a year ago I more or less suddenly realized that I have spent my whole professional life as an international economist thinking and writing about economic geography, without being aware of it.

By "economic geography" I mean "the location of production in space"; that is, that branch of economics that worries about where things happen in relation to one another. It's not worth trying to define my subject more exactly than that—you'll see better what I mean once I start describing models. Most of regional economics, and some but not all of urban economics, is about economic geography in the sense I have in mind.

If you had never looked at the theory of international trade, you might have supposed that international economics would also be largely treated as a special case of economic geography, one in which borders and the actions of sovereign governments play a special role in shaping the location of production. What I will argue in these lectures is that that is how international economics ought to be done, at least part of the time. But it is almost never the way that it is done at present. Instead, the analysis of international trade makes virtually no use of insights from economic geography or location theory. We normally model countries as dimensionless points within which factors of production can be instantly and costlessly moved from one activity to another, and even trade among countries is usually given a sort of spaceless representation in which transport costs are zero for all goods that can be traded.

There is nothing wrong with simplifying assumptions—on the contrary, it is only through strategic simplification that we can hope to make any sense of the buzzing complexity of the real world. The particular simplifying assumptions of conventional trade theory have led to an impressive and very useful intellectual construct. For some purposes it does no harm to ignore the fact that countries are not points and that some pairs of countries are much closer than others—that California is farther from New York than any place in the European Community is from any place else, or that London and Paris are much closer to each other than are New York and Chicago, or for that matter that Canada is essentially closer to the United States than it is to itself.

Yet the tendency of international economists to turn a blind eye to the fact that countries both occupy and exist in space—a tendency so deeply entrenched that we rarely even realize we are doing it—has, I would submit, had some serious costs. These lie not so much in lack of realism—all economic analysis is more or less unrealistic—as in the exclusion of important issues and, above all, of important sources of evidence. As I hope I will be able to show, one of the best ways to understand how the international economy works is to start by looking at what happens *inside* nations. If we want to understand differences in national growth rates, a good place to start is by examining differences in regional growth; if we want to understand international specialization, a good place to start is with local specialization. The data will be better and pose fewer problems of compatibility, and the underlying economic forces will be less distorted by government policies.

The decision by international economists to ignore the fact that they are doing geography wouldn't matter so much if someone else were busy exploiting the facts and insights that can come from looking at localization and trade within countries. Unfortunately, nobody is. That is, of course, an unfair statement. There are excellent economic geographers out there, as well as urban and regional economists who worry about geographical issues. For reasons that I will discuss in a moment, however, these people are almost uniformly peripheral to the economics profession. International economics is a flagship field: no serious economics department can get by without at least one international trade expert and without offering international economics as a field for its graduate students. By contrast, regional and even urban economics are given far less priority. And economic geographers proper are almost never found in economics departments, or even talking to economists; at best they are in urban studies departments, more usually in geography departments. They may do excellent work, but it does not inform or influence the economics profession.

There are good reasons why this has happened and equally good reasons why it should change. Before I begin to present my own ideas, I want to talk briefly about why international economists don't acknowledge that they are doing geography—and why they should.

Geography: Why Not and Why

The neglect of spatial issues in economics arises for the most part from one simple problem: how to think about market structure. Essentially, to say anything useful or interesting about the location of economic activity in space, it is necessary to get away from the constant-returns, perfect-competition approach that still dominates most economic analysis. As long as economists lacked the analytical tools to think rigorously about increasing returns and imperfect competition, the study of economic geography was condemned to lie outside the mainstream of the profession. Indeed, as standards of rigor in economics have risen over time, the study of location has been pushed further and further into the intellectual periphery.[1]

---

1. A major exception is urban economics, where there is a strong modeling tradition that informs a large body of empirical work. Henderson (1974, 1988), in particular, has developed a very persuasive framework for analyzing the evolution of an urban system and has provided extensive empirical evidence in support. I think it is fair to say, however, that international economists have largely ignored or been unaware of this body of work.

Not all students of economic geography have understood this. Much of the literature on industrial location, in particular, has ignored the issue of market structure and instead been obsessed with geometry—with the shape of market areas on an idealized landscape, or with the optimal siting of facilities given markets and resources—while paying little or no attention to the problem of modeling markets. This is, to my mind, doing things in the wrong order, worrying about the details of a secondary problem before making progress on the main issue.

Step back and ask, what is the most striking feature of the geography of economic activity? The short answer is surely *concentration*. Think of the United States: most of the population of a huge, fertile country lives along parts of two coasts and the Great Lakes; within these belts, population is further concentrated in a relative handful of densely populated urban areas. As I will document in the next lecture, these urban areas in turn are highly specialized, so that production in many industries is remarkably concentrated in space.

This geographic concentration of production is clear evidence of the pervasive influence of some kind of increasing returns. And there is the problem. Increasing returns are simply harder to model than constant or diminishing returns. If the increasing returns are purely external to firms, we can still use the tools of competitive analysis; but external economies turn out to be both analytically awkward and empirically elusive. If the

increasing returns are internal to firms, we are faced with the
necessity of modeling imperfect competition.

Economics tends, understandably, to follow the line of least
mathematical resistance. We like to explain the world in terms
of forces that we know how to model, not in terms of those we
don't. In international economics, what this meant from
Ricardo until the 1980s was an almost exclusive emphasis on
comparative advantage, rather than increasing returns, as an
explanation for trade.[2] The point was that comparative advantage could be modeled using models that assumed constant
returns and competition, which were the tools at hand. The
profession simply put those aspects of international trade that
could not be modeled that way on one side.

Unfortunately, the evident importance of increasing returns
in economic geography is so great that this understandable
impulse to focus on what we know how to deal with has led to
an avoidance of the subject as a whole. After 1940, in particular, as the expected level of rigor in economic discussion
steadily rose, economic geography was simply submerged.

But times have changed. During the 1970s there was a new
wave of theory in industrial organization, which provided the
economics profession with a menu of models of imperfect

---

2. For those who worry about definitions, by comparative advantage I mean
the general idea that countries trade in order to take advantage of their
differences. The increasing returns approach asserts instead that countries
trade because there are inherent advantages to specialization, even for initially similar countries.

competition. No one of these models is totally convincing, but they make it possible to write down coherent, rigorous, and often elegant models of economies subject to increasing returns. So increasing returns are no longer something to be avoided or assumed away at all costs. The new intellectual opportunities offered by this revolution in theory have in turn transformed a series of other fields. In international economics the past decade has seen a virtually complete rethinking, with the emergence of a new view in which much trade represents arbitrary specialization based on increasing returns, rather than an effort to take advantage of exogenous differences in resources or productivity.[3] More recently, growth theorists have reintroduced the idea that sustained growth may arise from the presence of increasing returns, and old concepts like the "big push" have regained intellectual respectability.[4] And very recently some macroeconomists have suggested that increasing returns play a crucial role in business cycles.[5]

I believe that the time has come to use the same new tools to resurrect economic geography as a major field within economics. It is no longer the case that the need to model increasing returns makes a field untouchable. Instead, increasing returns are, for the moment at least, actually fashionable. And

---

3. See Helpman and Krugman 1985 for a survey of most of the concepts of the "new international economics."
4. See in particular Romer 1986, 1987, 1990 and Murphy, Schleifer, and Vishny 1989a.
5. See Hall 1989 and also Murphy, Schleifer, and Vishny 1989b.

so we can now admit to ourselves that space matters and try to bring geography back into economic analysis.

There are three reasons in particular why it is important to start doing economic geography. First, the location of economic activity within countries is an important subject in its own right. Certainly for a large country like the United States, the allocation of production between regions is an issue as important as international trade—and more important than many issues that occupy a much larger part of economists' time. (I have my favorite candidates, but I won't tell you what they are; I have to live with these people for the next thirty years.)

Second, the lines between international economics and regional economics are becoming blurred in some important cases. One need only mention 1992 in Europe: as Europe becomes a unified market, with free movement of capital and labor, it will make less and less sense to think of the relations between its component nations in terms of the standard paradigm of international trade. Instead the issues will be those of regional economics—and it will help if we actually have some interesting regional economics to offer when the time comes.

To my mind, however, the most important reason to look again at economic geography is the intellectual and empirical laboratory that it provides. The "new" trade, growth, and business cycle theories of the past decade have suggested to us a world view of economics that is very different from that of most pre-1980 theory. Pervasive increasing returns and imperfect competition; multiple equilibria everywhere; an often decisive role for history, accident, and perhaps sheer self-fulfilling prophecy: these are the kind of ideas that are now becoming popular. Yet it is very difficult to produce compelling evidence from trade, growth, and business cycles that this is the way the world really works. I at least am convinced that there is a strong arbitrary, accidental component to international specialization; but not everyone agrees, and the limitations of the data make a decisive test difficult. Paul Romer is convinced that increasing returns play a large role in explaining sustained growth; but not everyone agrees, and even I am agnostic. Robert Hall thinks that increasing returns play a crucial role in business cycles (he argues that a city and a boom are essentially the same thing—one in space, one in time); not everyone agrees, and I for one find this totally implausible (but interesting!).

But when one turns to the location of production within countries, the evidence for what Nicholas Kaldor called "the irrelevance of equilibrium economics" is far more compelling. The long shadow cast by history and accident over the location of production is apparent at all scales, from the smallest to the largest—from the concentration of most U.S. manufacture of wind musical instruments in the tiny town of Elkhart, Indiana, to the fact that a third of the U.S. population still lives within the original thirteen colonies. And this clear dependence on history is the most convincing evidence available that we live in an economy closer to Kaldor's vision of a dynamic world driven by cumulative processes than to the standard constant-returns model.

What I want to do in this lecture is to offer a first illustration of the importance of economic geography, both as a field in its own right and as a way to see what kind of economy we live in. In particular, I want to show two things: that increasing returns are in fact a pervasive influence on the economy, and that these increasing returns give a decisive role to history in determining the geography of real economies.

I have already suggested that increasing returns affect economic geography at many scales. At the bottom of the scale, the location of particular industries—autos in Detroit, chips in Silicon Valley—clearly often reflects the "locking in" of transitory advantages. At an intermediate level, the existence of cities themselves is evidently an increasing returns phenomenon. At the grand level, the uneven development of whole regions (which in the United States may well be bigger than European nations) can be driven by cumulative processes that have increasing returns at their root.

In this lecture series I will pass over the question of urbanization relatively lightly. It has been better studied than the other issues I will consider (urban economics is more of an accepted field than economic geography), and it is also less relevant than the other aspects to international trade, which remains my ultimate interest. So I will focus on the small and the large:

the localization of particular industries and the differential development of huge regions. Today we look at the large, next lecture on the small.

To introduce the subject of divergent regional development, I turn to economic history to provide a particularly clear-cut example of the forces of economic geography at work. I then offer a simple model that helps make sense of that example. The example is the case of the U.S. "manufacturing belt": a relatively narrow stretch of territory within which the preponderance of U.S. manufacturing was concentrated from the mid–nineteenth century until the 1960s. The model—which is here developed only sketchily—is one in which the interaction of demand, increasing returns, and transportation costs drives a cumulative process of regional divergence.

The Case of the U.S. Manufacturing Belt

Early in this century, geographers noted that the great bulk of U.S. manufacturing was concentrated in a relatively small part of the Northeast and the eastern part of the Midwest—roughly speaking, within the approximate parallelogram Green Bay—St. Louis—Baltimore—Portland (figure 1.1). This "manufacturing belt"[6] took shape in the second half of the nineteenth

---

6. The term was apparently first used by DeGeer (1927). The belt is not unique, nor are the forces that established it confined to national boundaries. Industrial Canada, concentrated in part of Ontario, is essentially a part of the U.S. manufacturing belt. Continental Europe has a "manufacturing triangle" containing the Ruhr, Northern France, and Belgium that is a close cousin of the U.S. belt.

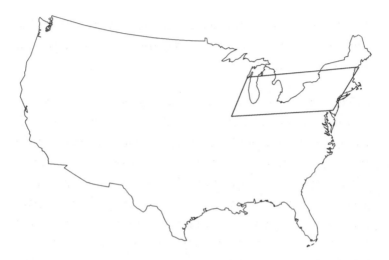

Figure 1.1

century and proved remarkably persistent. Perloff et al. (1960) estimated that as late as 1957 the manufacturing belt still contained 64 percent of U.S. manufacturing employment— only slightly reduced from its 74 percent share at the turn of the century.

Even this number understates the manufacturing dominance of this region, because during the heyday of the belt most of the manufacturing outside it consisted either of processing of primary products or of production for a very local market. That is, the manufacturing belt contained virtually all manufacturing that was "footloose," not tied to other locations either by the need to be very close to the consumer or by the need to use natural resources very close to their source.

Why did the manufacturing belt play such a dominant role for so long? It was clearly not a case of an enduring advantage in natural resources: the manufacturing belt persisted even as the center of gravity of agricultural and mineral production shifted far to the west. In 1870 the Northeast and East North Central regions—within which the emerging manufacturing belt lay—accounted for 44 percent of U.S. "resource extraction" employment (agriculture, mining, forestry, fisheries). By 1910 this share had already fallen to 27 percent; yet these regions still accounted for 70 percent of manufacturing employment. And whereas the belt's share of manufacturing employment understates its manufacturing dominance, its share of resource employment overstates its resource base. The reason is that much of the agriculture that took place within or near to the manufacturing belt was quite different from that outside it: it consisted largely of truck farming and dairying, existing less because of the suitability of the land than because of proximity to the urban centers. In other words, if the manufacturing belt had not existed, the Northeast and Great Lakes areas would have had an even smaller share of agricultural employment.

H. H. McCarty, writing during the belt's heyday, summarized the divergence between regions bluntly: "Outside the manufacturing belt, cities exist to serve the farms; inside, farms exist to serve the cities."

As for mineral resources, the manufacturing belt originally drew some of its critical raw materials from nearby coal mines and oil wells. By the mid–twentieth century, however, the great bulk of the raw materials for manufactures were imported from other regions.

Why, then, did so much of U.S. manufacturing stay within this relatively small stretch of territory? The answer in broad terms is, of course, obvious: each individual manufacturing facility stayed within the manufacturing belt because of the advantages of being near other manufacturers. And the apparent incentive for manufacturers to cluster together explains the persistence of the manufacturing belt even after the bulk of U.S. primary production had shifted to other regions. Once the belt had been established, it was not in the interest of any individual producer to move out of it.

One may ask why this geographical concentration became established in the first place—a question about historical specifics to which I will return below. First, however, let us ask the more fundamental question: what were the forces that led manufacturers to want to cluster together? I will sketch out a simple model in which geographical concentration results from demand externalities. This surely does not capture the full story, but it is strongly suggestive of the kind of explanation that is needed.

A Model of Geographic Concentration

The basic story of geographic concentration that I will propose here relies on the interaction of increasing returns, transportation costs, and demand.[7] Given sufficiently strong economies of scale, each manufacturer wants to serve the national market from a single location. To minimize transportation costs, she chooses a location with large local demand. But local demand will be large precisely where the majority of manufacturers choose to locate. Thus there is a circularity that tends to keep a manufacturing belt in existence once it is established.[8]

Imagine a country in which there are only two possible locations of production, East and West, and two kinds of production. Agricultural goods are produced using a location-specific factor (land), and as a result the agricultural population is exogenously divided between the locations; for the moment we assume that the division is fifty-fifty.

Manufactured goods (of which there are many symmetric varieties) can be produced in either or both locations. If a given manufactured good is produced in only one location, transportation costs must be incurred to service the other market. On the other hand, if the good is to be produced in both

---

7. This lecture presents only a sketch of a model. It will be apparent that this sketch is sloppy about a number of issues, including, What is the market structure in manufacturing? What happens to profits, if any? and What resources are used in both fixed costs and transportation? It is possible to derive similar results in a fully specified general equilibrium monopolistic competition model; such a model is presented in appendix A. I adopt the more ad hoc approach here for ease of exposition.

8. In this model I stress the role of demand in determining the location of production of goods that are traded interregionally. An alternative approach would stress the role of increasing returns in the production of nontraded goods, as in Faini 1984. Eventually deciding between approaches will have to be an empirical matter; but for now it is a matter of taste.

locations, an additional fixed setup cost is incurred. The manufacturing labor force in each location is proportional to manufacturing production in that location. Finally, assume that the demand for each manufactured good in each location is strictly proportional to that location's population.

The basic idea can then be illustrated with a simple numerical example. Suppose that 60 percent of a country's labor force are farmers, divided equally between East and West. Suppose also that the total demand for a typical manufactured good is 10 units. Then if all manufacturing is concentrated in one location, that location will demand 7 units (3 demanded by the local farmers, 4 by the manufacturing workers), while the other demands 3; if manufacturing is evenly divided between the locations, each location will offer a local demand of 5.

To figure out what happens, we need to specify the fixed costs and transportation costs; suppose that the fixed cost of opening a plant is 4, and that the transportation cost per unit is 1. Then we have the situation shown in table 1.1. The table shows the costs to a typical firm of three locational strategies, contingent on the locational strategies of all other firms. Thus suppose that all other manufacturing is concentrated in East. Then our firm will have a local demand in East of 7 units, a local demand in West of only 3 units. If it serves the national market from a single plant in East, it will incur a fixed cost of 4 and a transport cost of 3. This is obviously less than serving the national market from a plant in West, which will have the same

Table 1.1
A manufacturing location story

Distribution of manufacturing employment	Costs of typical firm if it produces in			
		East	Both	West
East only	Fixed	4	8	4
	Transportation	3	0	7
	Total	7	8	11
Fifty-fifty split	Fixed	4	8	4
	Transportation	5	0	5
	Total	9	8	9
West only	Fixed	4	8	4
	Transportation	7	0	3
	Total	11	8	7

fixed cost plus a transport cost of 7; it is also less than building a plant to serve each local market, which saves the transport cost but incurs a double fixed cost of 8. In this case, then, the typical firm will choose to produce in East for a national market.

If each firm concentrates its production in East, however, then manufacturing production as a whole will be concentrated in East—which is what is assumed. So concentration of production in East is an equilibrium.

But it is not the only equilibrium. As the rest of the table shows, if manufacturing is concentrated in West, each firm will similarly also want to concentrate its production in West. And if production is split between East and West, each firm will want to split its production, too. So in fact all three distributions of production—all in East, all in West, and a fifty-fifty split—are equilibria in this example.

The possibility of multiple equilibria can also be seen graphically (figure 1.2). On the horizontal axis we measure the share of the manufacturing labor force employed in West, on the vertical axis the share of West in the total population. The line MM represents the dependence of the distribution of manufacturing on the distribution of population; the line PP the converse effect of manufacturing on population distribution.

Let's begin with PP. This line represents the relationship between manufacturing labor force employment and total population. Let π be the share of the total population engaged in manufacturing, let s_M be the share of the manufacturing labor force employed in West, and let s_N be West's share of the total population. West is home to half of the farmers, so that at

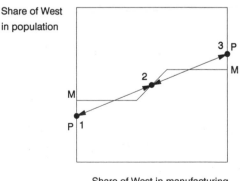

Share of West in manufacturing

Figure 1.2

minimum it has a population share of $(1-\pi)/2$. The more manufacturing it has, the larger this share:

$$s_N = \frac{1-\pi}{2} + \pi s_M.$$

This is an upward-sloping line that is, however, flatter than a 45-degree line.

Next turn to *MM*. Suppose that West has a very small share of the population. Then it will not be worthwhile incurring the fixed costs of establishing a manufacturing facility there; it is cheaper to serve the market from facilities in East. Conversely, if West has a very large share of the population, it is not worth producing manufactures in East. If the fixed cost is not too large relative to transportation costs, a sufficiently equal division of population will lead manufacturers to produce locally for both markets. Putting these observations together, we get the illustrated shape of *MM*: no Western production for low Western population, production proportional to population for intermediate levels, no Eastern production if the West is big enough. Let x be the sales of a typical manufacturing firm, F the fixed cost of opening a branch plant, and t the transportation cost of shipping a unit of manufactures from East to West or vice versa. Then it is cheaper to service West from a plant in East than to open a Western plant as long as $s_N xt < F$; it is cheaper to service East from West if $(1-s_N)xt < F$; and it is cheaper to have a plant in each region if neither is true.

Provided that fixed costs are not too high relative to transport costs,[9] we therefore have

$$s_M = 0 \ if \ s_N < \frac{F}{tx}$$

$$= s_N \ if \ \frac{F}{tx} < s_N < 1 - \frac{F}{tx}$$

$$= 1 \ if \ 1 - \frac{F}{tx} < s_N.$$

Suppose that manufacturing production adjusts gradually toward its equilibrium level. Then the dynamics are illustrated by the arrows in figure 1.2. There are three stable equilibria: manufacturing may be concentrated in either location, at 1 or 3, or it may be equally divided, at 2. Which equilibrium you get to depends on where you start: history matters.

Of course there need not be multiple equilibria. The concentration of production, if it happens, depends on a demand externality. Manufacturers want to locate where the market is largest; the market is largest where the manufacturers locate. This circularity, however, need not always be strong enough to prevail over the pull of the dispersed agricultural sector. The situation could instead look like figure 1.3: a unique, stable equilibrium with manufacturing equally divided between the two locations.

---

9. If $F > tx/2$, then it is always cheaper to service both markets from a single plant, even if the population is equally divided. In this case MM is simply a horizontal line, and the possibility of an equilibrium with equally divided manufacturing disappears.

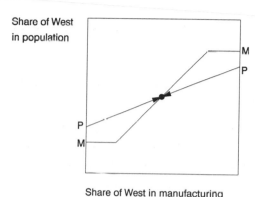

Figure 1.3

We can easily derive a necessary condition for concentration of manufacturing production in one location. With all manufacturing in East, West has a share of total population equal to only $(1-\pi)/2$. The transportation cost of serving this market from East for a typical manufacturer is therefore $tx(1-\pi)/2$. The cost of setting up a plant in West is F. So a concentration of production in East, once established, will persist as long as

$$F > \frac{1-\pi}{2} tx .$$

If this criterion is not met, history does not matter: the geography of manufactures will follow that of agriculture.

We can immediately see that a key role for history depends on three parameters: large F, i.e., sufficiently strong economies of scale; small t, i.e., sufficiently low costs of transportation; and large π, i.e., a sufficiently large share of "footloose" production not tied down by natural resources.

We can now tell a stylized story of the emergence of the manufacturing belt.[10] In the early United States, with its primarily agricultural population, where manufacturing was marked by few scale economies and where transportation was costly, no strong geographical concentration could occur. As the country began its industrial transition, manufacturing arose in areas that contained most of the agricultural population outside the South—and the South was, for reasons having to do with its uniquely awful institutions, unsuited for manufacturing. During the second half of the nineteenth century, however, manufacturing economies of scale increased,[11] transportation costs fell, and the share of the population in nonagricultural occupations rose. The result was that the initial advantage of the manufacturing belt was locked in. Even though new land and new resources were exploited to the west, even though slavery ended, for three-quarters of a

---

10. This story is based on the fascinating work of David Myers (1983), who however bears no responsibility for the crudity of the representation.

11. Chandler (1990) provides a fascinationg story of the emergence of large manufacturing firms in the period between the Civil War and the 1920s—that is, during the heyday of the manufacturing belt. He shows that in one industry after another, a "first-mover" led the way by taking advantage of new technology and lower transport costs to build one or two plants of unprecedented size, serving the whole national market. While Chandler does not emphasize the point, his U.S. firms invariably established their first huge plant somewhere inside the manufacturing belt. Sometimes this choice was dictated by the availability of specific resources—for example, hydroelectric power for aluminum smelters at Niagara Falls—but access to markets seems to have played a key role in ruling out sites outside the manufacturing belt.

century the pull of the established manufactured areas was strong enough to keep the manufacturing core virtually intact.

Of course this story oversimplifies in a number of ways. On one side, it probably underemphasizes the role of certain conventional factors in giving rise to the manufacturing belt—there is a suspicious correlation between the location of heavy industry and that of coalfields, both in the United States and in Europe. On the other side, it says nothing about the sources of local specialization within the manufacturing belt—about why Detroit emerged as the automotive center, New York as the garment center, Grand Rapids as the furniture center, etc. Yet it surely captures an important aspect of what happened. And it also contains elements—increasing returns at the level of individual firms, and external economies resulting from the interaction of these firms' decisions—that will reappear as one further elaborates the story.

Before changing the subject, however, there is one particular aspect of the rise of the manufacturing belt that deserves some further elaboration. This is the role of the endogeneity of transport costs themselves.

Transport Networks and Regional Divergence

It is obvious from even a cursory reading of U.S. economic history that part of the advantage of the manufacturing belt arose from the density of the railroad network connecting the region's cities, a density that was itself a product of the region's manufacturing dominance. This transport network effect deserves a little more attention.

Imagine for a moment a nation with not two but three locations—Center, West, and South—with equal transportation costs between any two locations. Where will a manufacturing firm locate? By analogy with our previous discussion, if one of these locations offers a sufficiently larger local market than the others, and if fixed costs are large enough relative to transport costs, the more populated location will attract a concentration of manufacturing production.

Now imagine a nation with *four* locations: East, Midwest, West, and South. But now suppose that the transportation cost between East and Midwest is much lower than that in other directions. Then in economic terms East and Midwest will in effect form a *single* location. The East-Midwest region will be a more attractive place to locate manufacturing than South or West, even if the individual markets are no bigger, because factories in either place will have better access to the combined market.

But why should transportation costs in one direction be much lower than in others? The most natural answer is that there are economies of scale in transportation itself. A railway or a highway represents indivisible investments, while the frequency of air service and the ability to use large, efficient planes depends on the volume of demand. Suppose that manufacturing production, and hence both demand and supply, is concentrated in East and Midwest. Then there will be a greater volume of transportation between these locations than on other routes. This will mean lower transport costs, which will in turn reinforce the advantage of East and Midwest as locations for production.

It is possible in principle to imagine this transportation network effect as an independent source of geographical concentration of industry—that is, to set up a model in which the local market size effect that is the driving force for our basic model is absent. In practice, of course, the two effects work together. The U.S. manufacturing belt was characterized not only by a denser population but also by a better transport network than any other part of the country, and thus offered much better market access to manufacturers.

Further Thoughts

The case of the U.S. manufacturing belt is of substantial interest in its own right. The rise and persistence of that belt is an important yet much neglected aspect of U.S. economic history. More important than its immediate significance, however, is what the history of manufacturing location says about the nature of our economy in general. And what it says is that increasing returns and cumulative processes are pervasive and give an often decisive role to historical accident.

It is also interesting that the story of the manufacturing belt reaches back to the mid–nineteenth century. It is common to argue, as Brian Arthur has, that external economies and cumulative processes have become more important in recent decades because of the growing importance of technology. The geographical concentration of manufacturing in the United States took shape, however, long before the dawn of the information age. So it is not simply true that our economy is not now well described by the conventional constant-returns model. It never was.

The Process of Change

The circular relationship in which the location of demand determines the location of production, and vice versa, can be a deeply conservative force, tending to lock into place any established center-periphery pattern. In the case of the U.S. manufacturing belt, the geographical structure of production that happened to exist at the point at which industrialization, factory production, and the railroad came into force remained essentially intact for the next century.

Nothing, however, is forever. Indeed, one of the most interesting things about the type of model sketched in this lecture is what is says about the process of economic change. What I want to do at this point is illustrate two ideas in particular that are suggested by the center-periphery model. First is that while the geographical structure of production may be stable for long periods of time, when it does change it may change rapidly. In fact, a gradual change in underlying conditions can at times lead to explosive, or more accurately, catastrophic change. Second, change when it comes may be influenced strongly not only by objective conditions but also by expectations—expectations that may be self-fulfilling.

The Logic of Sudden Change

To see how change in the geography of production can sometimes take place abruptly, suppose that instead of being divided equally between the locations, the agricultural labor force is unevenly split, with West initially having a smaller population. The hypothetical position is shown in figure 1.4. *PP* is the initial relationship between manufacturing employment and total population. Although a possible equilibrium exists at 2 in which West would produce manufactures, we suppose that owing to a head start for East we are instead at 1, with no manufacturing production in West.

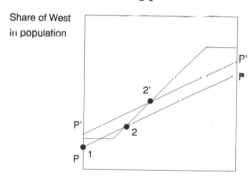

Share of West in population

Share of West in manufacturing

Figure 1.4

Now suppose that there is a gradual reallocation of the agricultural labor force from East to West. This will shift PP upward, toward $P'P'$. It is immediately obvious that at a certain point East's dominance of manufactures will collapse. When the Western population reaches a critical mass, it becomes worthwhile for manufacturers to produce there; as manufacturing production in West increases, the population rises further, stimulating still further increases in manufacturing production. A small increase in the agricultural base may therefore set in motion a cumulative process of import substitution and growth, leading eventually to an equilibrium at a point like 2'.

This scenario may not be entirely hypothetical. Paul Rhode (1988) has pointed out that late nineteenth-century California was a resource-based economy with limited manufacturing, largely because the local market was too small to support much industry. He suggests that the discovery of oil around the turn of the century raised California to critical mass, starting it on a process of explosive growth (and in particular causing the rapid emergence of Los Angeles as a manufacturing center).

The point is that the same kind of model that helps explain why history matters also suggests that when change does come, it will often be sudden. And we may also note that changes in regional fortunes will be difficult to predict: in the hypothetical history illustrated in figure 1.4 one would see a sudden acceleration in West's growth without any obvious reason.

History versus Expectations

Now that I have described the logic of sudden change, let me raise a problem with that logic—a problem that will no doubt already have occurred to those readers with a background in modern macroeconomics, with its emphasis on rationality of expectations. Suppose that the distribution of agricultural population were in fact evolving in the way illustrated in figure 1.4. Wouldn't manufacturing workers and/or firms realize that a sudden increase in West's population was in prospect? And wouldn't they begin to move into West in anticipation of that increase, thereby smoothing out the process of change?

The answer is yes, if they were sufficiently well informed. In practice I have my doubts—here as elsewhere, the assumption of rational expectations seems to presume a degree of information and sophistication that is unreasonable. That is not a controversy that I want to get too far into; I just want to argue that the kind of static expectations that implicitly underlies the dynamics in figure 1.4 retains a useful place in analysis.

But even if I am skeptical about the literal relevance of the assumption of rational expectations, now that we have raised the issue of the role of expectations in regional development, we should pursue it. For if you think about it a bit, you realize that the kind of circular process that I have argued leads to regional differentiation can also lead to self-fulfilling prophecies.

Imagine again our two-region nation; this time assume for simplicity that the economies of scale are sufficiently large relative to transport costs that there are only two long-run equilibria, with manufacturing concentrated either entirely in East or entirely in West. Suppose, however, that workers cannot all move at once; that there is some kind of adjustment cost that limits the rate at which manufacturing can shift. Thus a worker who chooses to locate in one region or the other is stuck with that choice, at least for a while.

It is immediately apparent that in this case workers will be concerned with more than their current wage—they will base their decisions to move on something like the present value of future wages. But the real wage rates in each region at any point in time depend on the distribution of manufacturing workers; so this means that each worker's current location decision depends on her expectations about the future decisions of other workers.

The possibility of self-fulfilling prophecy now becomes apparent. Suppose that East and West have equal numbers of farmers, and that East initially has somewhat more manufacturing, so that by virtue of its superior forward and backward linkages East offers a higher real manufacturing wage. Then one might expect to see migration of manufacturing from West to East. But suppose that for some reason the public is convinced that West will be the destination of migration, not East, and that as a result real wages in West will eventually exceed those in East. This belief will induce seemingly perverse migration from the region with higher real wages to that with lower—and this migration will indeed eventually reverse the real wage differential! And if this reversal takes place sufficiently quickly, the worker who migrates from East to West will find that she actually made the right decision. Thus the belief that West is the land of opportunity turns out to be a self-fulfilling prophecy. If everyone had instead had faith in the East, of course, East would have gotten the industry.

When can self-fulfilling prophecy outweigh initial advantage? Several factors clearly matter. First, the rate at which workers and firms can move must be rapid enough relative to the rate at which future wage differentials are discounted that the future advantage of one region can matter more than the current advantage of another. Second, increasing returns must be strong enough that an expected future shift in population distribution moves the real wage differential quickly. Finally, the starting position must not be too unequal: if enough manufacturing is concentrated in one region, this initial advantage may be too much for even the most optimistic expectations about the other region to overcome.

It is possible to formalize the problem of self-fulfilling expectations rather neatly; such a formalization is presented in appendix B. What the formalization tells us is that there may be a range of initial distributions of manufacturing workers from which either region can end up with the manufacturing concentration, depending on expectations. Whether such a range exists, and the size of the range if it does exist, depend crucially on the speed of adjustment; only if the adjustment is slow can we be sure that initial advantage cumulates over time, instead of potentially being overruled by self-fulfilling expectations.

So much for the logic. To what, if anything, does this story correspond in reality? The answer is that I am not sure. In the case of the U.S. manufacturing belt, history clearly determined what happened. Perhaps there could have been a self-fulfilling belief in the industrial future of, say, the Great Plains that could have outweighed the historical advantage of the traditional manufacturing locations; but there wasn't. (And I doubt it.)

At a smaller scale, however, the case for self-fulfillment is better. Certainly a prominent part of the tradition of local economic development in the United States has been boosterism—the sometimes ludicrous efforts by local businessmen and chambers of commerce to convince footloose individuals and firms of the virtues of their state or town, in the belief that if they can draw a critical mass into the local economy, it will become self-sustaining. Some of this boosterism involved concrete incentives, sort of proto-industrial policy; we'll see an example in the story of Akron and the rubber industry in the next lecture. But often it was simply an attempt to create optimism about the locale. The analysis sketched out here suggests that in principle, at least, boosterism may make perfectly good sense.

There is also the possibility of reverse boosterism: if for some reasons businesses and workers become pessimistic about a region's prospects, this pessimism can become self-justifying. It is difficult for me to avoid speculating that something like this may be happening in my own home state. As you may know, two years ago the governor of Massachusetts ran for president, in part on the impressive economic record of his state. He was humiliatingly defeated by George Bush—and the Massachusetts economy itself went into a tailspin. Was this just a coincidence, or did the psychological impact of the campaign, and the political civil wars that followed within the state, create a self-fulfilling downward spiral? (And will the state's economy continue to implode?) I don't know the answer, but such seemingly fanciful ideas don't seem as silly to me as they might to a more conventionally minded economist.

Where We Stand

In this lecture I have tried to argue for the acceptance of economic geography as a major field within economics, on a par with or even in some sense encompassing the field of international trade. Since we all know that economic argumentation succeeds at least as much on its aesthetics as its empirical support, I have tried to make my case with the cutest model of geography that I have been able to come up with: one that shows how a core-periphery structure can emerge endogenously on a nationwide scale. And I have argued that something like this actually happened in the United States between the Civil War and the First World War.

The phenomenon of concentration in economic geography takes place at many scales, however. While the emergence of huge metropolitan belts may be the most dramatic, for international affairs the forces that lead to localization of particular industries, usually but not always within those belts, are possibly of even more interest. So in the next lecture I will move from the large to the small: from core-periphery to localization.

2   Localization

In 1895 a teenaged girl named Catherine Evans, living in the small Georgia city of Dalton, made a bedspread as a wedding gift. It was an unusual bedspread for the time, in that it was tufted; the craft of tufting or candlewicking had been common in the eighteenth and early nineteenth centuries but had fallen into disuse by that time. As a direct consequence of that wedding gift, Dalton emerged after World War II as the preeminent carpet manufacturing center of the United States. Six of the top twenty U.S. carpet manufacturing firms are located in Dalton; all but one of the rest are located nearby, and the carpet industry in Dalton and vicinity employs nineteen thousand workers.

I'll come back to Catherine Evans and her story later in this lecture. For now let me simply assert that aside from being particularly charming, the carpet story is actually a fairly typical one. To a remarkable extent, manufacturing industries within the United States are highly localized; and when one tries to understand the reasons for that localization, one finds that it can be traced back to some seemingly trivial historical accident.

I'll tell some stories later. First, let's develop an analytical structure.

Sources of Industry Localization

The observation of high localization of industries is, of course, not a new one. Indeed, it was such a striking feature of the process of industrialization that it attracted a great deal of attention in the later nineteenth century, with a fascinating monograph on the subject contained in the 1900 U.S. Census. The literature on industry localization is much too extensive to cite; notable examples over the years include Hoover 1948, Lichtenberg 1960, and very recently, Porter 1990. There is also considerable overlap between the subject of industry localization and urban economics; theory, anecdotal evidence, and solid empirical work can be found in such works as Bairoch 1988, Jacobs 1969 and 1984, and Henderson 1988.

Let us, however, go back to the source. It was Alfred Marshall who presented the classic economic analysis of the phenomenon. (Actually, it was the observation of industry localization that underlay Marshall's concept of external economies, which makes the modern neglect of the subject even more surprising.)

Marshall (1920) identified three distinct reasons for localization. First, by concentrating a number of firms in an industry in the same place, an industrial center allows a pooled market for workers with specialized skills; this pooled market benefits both workers and firms:

[A] localized industry gains a great advantage from the fact that it offers a constant market for skill. Employers are apt to resort to any place where they are likely to find a good choice of workers with the special skill which they require; while men seeking employment naturally go to places where there are many employers who need such skill as theirs and where therefore it is likely to find a good market. The owner of an isolated factory, even if he has good access to a plentiful supply of general labor, is often put to great shifts for want of some special skilled labor; and a skilled workman, when thrown out of employment in it, has no easy refuge.

Second, an industrial center allows provision of nontraded inputs specific to an industry in greater variety and at lower cost:

[S]ubsidiary trades grow up in the neighborhood, supplying it with implements and materials, organizing its traffic, and in many ways conducing to the economy of its material...the economic use of expensive machinery can sometimes be attained in a very high degree in a district in which there is a large aggregate production of the same kind, even though no individual capital employed in the trade be very large. For subsidiary industries devoting themselves each to one small branch of the process of production, and working it for a great many of their neighbors, are able to keep in constant use machinery of the most highly specialized character, and to make it pay its expenses. . .

Finally, because information flows locally more easily than over greater distances, an industrial center generates what we would now call technological spillovers:

The mysteries of the trade become no mystery; but are as it were in the air. . . . Good work is rightly appreciated, inventions and improvements in machinery, in processes and the general organization of the business have their merits promptly discussed: if one man starts a new idea, it is taken up by others and combined with suggestions of their own; and thus it becomes the source of further new ideas.

(On the whole, I like Marshall's turn of phrase better than the modern one!)

Cut through the archaism of Marshall's language and his lack of formalism, and you will see that he had a pretty sophisticated model in mind. He missed a few tricks that I will try to point out, but on the whole the main purpose of this part of the lecture is to rephrase Marshall in a drier, less felicitous style, and thereby bring it up to date.

Let us therefore consider in turn each of the Marshallian reasons for localization.

Labor Market Pooling

Imagine for a moment that there is some industry that consists of just two firms, each of which can produce in either of only two locations. These firms both use the same distinctive kind of skilled labor. For whatever reason, however, the firms' demands for labor are not perfectly correlated. For example, they may produce differentiated products that face uncertain demand; or they may be subject to firm-specific production shocks. Whatever the reason, the labor demand of the firms is both uncertain and imperfectly correlated.

To make matters more concrete, suppose that each firm may experience either "good times," in which it would like to hire 125 specialized workers at the going wage, or "bad times," in which it would like to hire only 75. We also suppose that there are 200 of these workers in total, so that average demand for labor equals supply. (In this example I take the wage rate for the specialized labor as given, so that there may be either excess demand or excess supply for labor. If you like, imagine a wage bargaining process that sets the wage at an expected market-clearing level before the shocks to labor demand are revealed—not too unrealistic an assumption. This assumption is not, however, essential. I will show in a moment that even if the wage rate is completely flexible and the labor market clears, the basic story remains the same.)

Now we may ask: will firms and workers be better off if the two firms choose different locations—each thus forming a company town with a local labor force of 100—or if the two firms choose the same location, with a pooled labor force of 200 that can work at either firm?

You may immediately ask about the possibility of exploitation: wouldn't each firm prefer to have a captive local labor force? I'll come back to that soon and show that it doesn't work the way you may think. For now, just put it aside and assume that the wage is set at an expected market-clearing level. Then it should immediately be apparent that it is in the interest of both firms and workers that everyone be in the same place.

First, consider the situation from firms' point of view. If each has its own town, with a labor force of 100, then it will be unable to take advantage of its good fortune when labor demand is high: during good times, there will be an unfillable excess demand of 25 workers. If the two firms are in the same place, however, then at least occasionally one firm's good times will coincide with the other firm's bad times, and there will be additional workers available.

Next consider the situation from workers' point of view. If they live in a company town, then the firm's bad times are their bad times too: whenever the firm has low labor demand, 25 workers will be laid off. If the firms are in the same place, then at least sometimes one firm's bad times will be offset by the other firm's good times, and the average rate of unemployment will correspondingly be lower.

This is a pretty trivial example. Yet I think it is useful as a way to clear up some points that are often misunderstood. First, the example clarifies the nature of the gains from labor market pooling. Because of the word "pooling" some people may be tempted to assume that the incentive to create a pooled labor market is something like portfolio diversification, that is, that it has something to do with risk aversion on the part of workers. No doubt minimizing risk is also an issue, but I didn't mention it in the example. So even if workers were entirely risk-neutral, there would be an efficiency gain from creating a localized industry with a pooled labor market.

Second, if you think about it, the example shows that uncertainty alone won't generate localization. You need increasing returns as well. The key point is that in order to make a pooled labor market advantageous, I needed to assume that each firm had to choose one location or the other, not both. If each firm could produce in both locations, or for that matter if each firm could be split into two identical firms, one in each place, then the full "portfolio" of firms and workers could be replicated in each location, and the motivation for localization would be gone. But the most natural justification for the assumption that firms do not locate in both places is that there are sufficient economies of scale to militate for a single production site.

So it is the *interaction* of increasing returns and uncertainty that makes sense of Marshall's labor pooling argument for localization. But as I have described it so far, it is only an argument for the advantage of concentrated production, not a description of the process that might bring about such concentration. Can we provide such a description?

Consider figure 2.1 (which bears more than a coincidental resemblance to some of the figures from the last lecture). I envision an industry in which there are a fixed number of firms

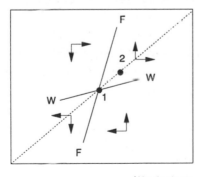

West's share
of workers

Figure 2.1

and a limited supply of specialized workers. Each firm and each worker must choose one of two locations, East or West. On the horizontal axis I show West's share of the labor force, on the vertical axis its share of the number of firms.

Which location will firms and workers prefer? The curves *FF* and *WW* show which distributions of firms and workers will leave the typical firm and worker respectively indifferent between the two locations. Both curves cross the 45-degree line at point 1, in the middle of the box: if everything is the same, everything is the same.

For any given labor force, firms would rather face less competition for the available workers. Thus an increase in the share of firms in West will make that location less attractive for the typical firm, unless this increase is offset by an increase in the labor force as well. So the set of combinations of share of firms and share of labor force that leaves firms indifferent between the locations, shown by *FF*, is upward sloping.

Workers would prefer to share the demand of any given number of firms with as few other workers as possible; an increase in the labor force in West will therefore make it a less attractive location for workers, unless offset by an increase in the number of firms. So the set of combinations of share of firms and share of labor force that leaves workers indifferent between East and West, shown by *WW*, is also upward sloping.

As drawn, *FF* is steeper than *WW*. To see why, consider point 2. At that point, the ratio of firms to workers is the same in West and East; but West has more of both. This means that West will offer better labor market pooling, and hence that at point 2 both firms and workers will prefer West to East. So point 2 is below FF (West is preferred by firms) and above WW (West is preferred by workers). This is only possible if at point 1 FF is steeper than WW.

Now ask what happens if we are off these schedules of equal attractiveness. Presumably firms move to the more attractive location, as do workers. The resulting dynamics are illustrated by the arrows in figure 2.1. There are three equilibria; but the one in the middle is knife-edge unstable. So we will converge to concentration of both firms and workers either in East or West, depending on initial conditions.[1]

This is a rough formalization of Marshall's labor pooling argument. It has many loose ends, of course; let me try to tie up a few of them.

Additional Thoughts on Labor Pooling
The biggest loose end in the story just told—a loose end that is flapping free in Marshall as well—is in the description of wage determination. In fact, this is a double issue (a split loose end?). First, how dependent is the argument on the assumption of sticky wages and a non-clearing labor market? Second, what

---

1. Obviously there is an issue of self-fulfilling prophecy, of expectations as opposed to history, in models of localization as well as in the more macro model of the previous lecture. I will take it as understood that this issue is lurking in the background, and proceed with ad hoc dynamics that ignore the expectational problem.

about the issue of exploitation—the advantage to firms of a monopsony position in a company town?

A special example can help demonstrate that even with flexible wages it is advantageous to have a pooled labor force. Return to our two-firm example, but now suppose that each firm has a downward-sloping demand for labor rather than a simple number of workers that it wants. Let wages be flexible, and ignore the potential for monopsony. Then in the case where the firms locate in different places there will no longer be unemployment or excess demand for labor; instead, the local wage rate will fluctuate.

If the firms formed a pooled labor market, however, the wage rate would fluctuate less. Risk-averse workers would like this. But beyond this, firms would find that their profits were higher. To see this, take the extreme case in which the labor demands of the two firms are perfectly negatively correlated, so that the wage rate in the pooled case does not fluctuate at all. The average wage rate would be the same[2]; but this does not leave the firms indifferent.

Consider figure 2.2. It shows the "good times" and "bad times" labor demands of one of the two firms. If the firm is isolated, it pays a high good-times wage and a low bad-times wage, while always employing the same number of people; if it is part of a pooled market, it pays a constant wage that is the average of the two. But it now employs more workers in good

---

2. Actually, to leave the average wage rate unchanged we must assume both linearity of the labor demand schedules and additivity of the shocks; but the basic point goes through regardless, as shown in appendix C.

wage

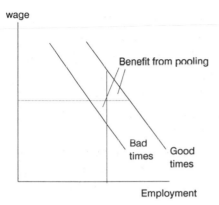

Figure 2.2

times, fewer in bad. As a result, the gain to the firm from the lower wage it pays in good times is greater than the loss it suffers from the higher wage it pays in bad times. In the figure, the net benefit is measured by the sum of the areas of the two indicated triangles.

This is an extreme example, but it makes a more general point. The gains from labor pooling do not rest in any essential way on a failure of labor markets to clear.

What about monopsony power? Won't firms prefer to have a captive labor force that they can exploit? Yes, other things equal. But other things won't be equal—and in fact the monopsony issue actually acts as a further reason for localization.[3]

---

3. This point was first made by Julio Rotemberg and Garth Saloner (1990). The style of their model is very different from what I present here, but essentially I am just offering a variant of their analysis.

To see why, now let us eliminate the uncertainty motive for pooling, and suppose that firms have known labor demand schedules. They will ordinarily, however, be off these schedules, because they will restrict their hiring in an effort to keep wages down. The extent of this restriction will depend on the degree of competition among the firms, which will presumably depend on how many firms there are in each location.[4] So an equal proportional increase in the number of firms and workers will benefit workers, hurt firms. So in figure 2.3, which has the same format as figure 2.1, both FF and WW are shown as flatter than the 45-degree line.

But I show FF as steeper than WW. That is, an increase in West's share of the labor force, offset by a large enough increase in its share of firms to leave workers indifferent between East and West, will make West a more attractive location for firms.

To see why, compare points 1 and 2 in the figure. At point 1, which is the middle of the box, both wage rates and the profits of a typical firm are the same in East and West. At point 2, where West has a larger labor force offset by a larger number of firms, wage rates are still the same— so workers are still indifferent. However, firms are more profitable in West, even though they pay the same wage, because they engage in less restriction of hiring in order to keep the wage down. Because

4. Formulating the nature of competition in the labor market is tricky. Rotemberg and Saloner assume Bertrand competition, so that the wage goes from the reservation wage to the competitive level when the number of firms goes from one to two. This seems a little extreme; as appendix C points out, however, it is difficult to come up with an equally elegant alternative. For the purposes of this exercise I will simply assume that exploitation goes down as the number of firms rises.

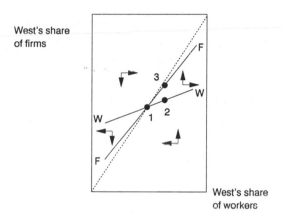

West's share
of firms

West's share
of workers

Figure 2.3

the number of firms has not risen in proportion to the number
of workers, each firm has larger employment; since workers
are paid less than their marginal product, this means higher
profits. So in order to leave firms indifferent between West and
East, it would be necessary to offset the increase in West's labor
force by a larger increase in the number of firms, for example
at point 3. Thus we know that FF, while flatter than the 45-
degree line, is steeper than WW.

Once again the dynamics are illustrated by the arrows; and we
see that the equilibrium in the middle is unstable, and the
industry ends up concentrating either in East or in West. But
in this example we have assumed away uncertainty, so that
there are no pooling gains from concentrating the industry.
Instead, the concentration of the industry is driven entirely by
the issue of market power in the labor market. The intuitive
argument that says that firms prefer company towns, because
of the monopsony power this gives them, is exactly wrong.

Why does it turn out this way? One way to think about it is the following: there is a tug-of-war between firms, who prefer a less competitive labor market and hence production in both locations, and workers, who prefer a more competitive market and hence concentration in one location. Workers win this tug-of-war because a more competitive labor market is also more efficient; given noncollusive choice of location by firms, this efficiency gain decisively tips the scales toward the concentrated solution.

An alternative, and perhaps deeper, way to view the issue is in terms of credibility. Firms would like to convince workers that they will *not* try to exploit their monopsony power, so that they can attract workers to their production location.[5] But the only credible way to do this is to have enough firms in the location that there is an assurance of competition for workers. The commonsense idea that firms would like to have a company town in which workers could be exploited is right; but the point is that workers will shun such towns if they can, so that firms will end up finding it more profitable to locate in agglomerated centers that are not company towns.[6]

---

5. In Rotemberg and Saloner's formulation workers are not mobile, but immobile workers must choose whether or not to invest in industry-specific human capital. The basic principle is the same.

6. Of course company towns do exist. Impressionistically, they seem to happen for one of two reasons. First, there may be specific natural advantages that cause individual factories to be located on scattered sites, as was the case for water-driven New England textile towns. Second, the economies of scale in an industry may be so large that a single firm dominates the industry and agglomerates its plants in order to achieve pooling, like Eastman-Kodak in Rochester or Boeing in Seattle.

So it turns out that the loose ends that Marshall left in his labor market story do not invalidate it. Allowing for the possibility of flexible wage rates, while eroding some of the simplicity of the labor pooling story, does not make it go away; allowing for the possibility that firms may try to exploit monopsony power actually makes the story stronger.

Intermediate Inputs

Marshall's second reason for agglomeration, the availability of specialized inputs and services, seems straightforward enough. A localized industry can support more specialized local suppliers, which in turn makes that industry more efficient and reinforces the localization.

There are two points, however, that could perhaps use some clarification. First, the intermediate inputs story, like the labor pooling story, depends crucially on at least some degree of economies of scale. If there were no economies of scale in the production of intermediate inputs, then even a small-scale center of production could replicate a large one in miniature and still achieve the same level of efficiency. It is only the presence of increasing returns that makes a large center of production able to have more efficient and more diverse suppliers than a small one.

Second, the intermediate inputs story does not depend on some asymmetry in transportation costs between intermediate and final goods. Weber-type stories of transport cost minimization may suggest that localized industrial complexes will emerge only if it is more costly to transport intermediate inputs than final goods. This is an impression that may have been reinforced by some models in trade, unfortunately including the work of Elhanan Helpman and myself (1985). In our models of international trade we contrasted the case where intermediate goods are tradable but final goods are not—which gave rise in effect to external economies at the level of the world rather than the individual country— with the reverse, which led to the formation of national industrial complexes. The reason for stressing these two extreme cases was convenience: it is easier to model a good that is either perfectly tradable or perfectly nontradable than one that can be traded, but only at a cost. Unfortunately, this approach can convey the impression that localization due to the clustering of suppliers occurs only in the special case in which transportation costs for intermediate goods are particularly high.

This is a misleading impression. In fact, localization will tend to occur unless the costs of transporting intermediates are particularly *low* compared with those of transporting final goods. And a general reduction in transport costs, of both intermediates and final goods, will ordinarily tend to encourage localization rather than discourage it.

To see why, it is useful to consider a tricky sort of model in which intermediates and final goods are the same thing. Imagine a group of products each one of which is demanded both as a final good and as an input into all of the others. For example, suppose that the typical product in the group has total sales of 10, but that 4 of these sales are to manufacturers of other products in the group. And correspondingly we must suppose that to produce these 10 units requires 4 units of intermediate inputs, which again are drawn from the same industry. Notice that by making each good both a final and an intermediate, I have a fortiori imposed symmetry among intermediates and final goods in terms of their tradability.

Now suppose that there are two possible locations of production, each of which is also the location of half the final demand, that is, 3 units of each product. Where will a firm want to locate? The answer obviously depends on the decisions of other firms. If everyone else is in East, then 7 of the 10 units of total demand will be in East (3 final plus 4 intermediate); this will provide a firm with an incentive to locate its own production in East as well. The incentive will be reinforced by the fact that all of the firm's supplies of intermediate goods will come from East and will therefore be cheaper there. Thus there will be both backward and forward linkages that provide an incentive to concentrate production. Of course there will also be an incentive to move closer to final demand that will pull the other way.

This should be sounding familiar: it sounds an awful lot like the core-periphery model sketched out in the first lecture and derived formally in appendix A. And indeed it is possible to construct a model of intermediate goods and industry localization that is formally exactly analogous to the core-periphery model. This is helpful, because we already know something about that model. In particular, we know that the prospects for formation of a core-periphery pattern depend negatively on transportation costs, positively on the share of "foot-

loose" demand, and positively on the importance of economies of scale. The same should be true here, if these variables
are suitably reinterpreted. In particular, the role played by the
share of manufactures in the core-periphery model is here
taken instead by the share of the industry's output that is used
as an intermediate good rather than directly for final demand.
Given this, we see that lower transport costs make industrial
localization more likely, even if the cost of transporting intermediates falls along with that of transporting final goods.

It is also interesting to note that the same historical forces that
in the last lecture I argued gave rise in the nineteenth century
to the emergence of geographical concentration at a macro
level—falling transportation costs, industrialization, and growing economies of scale—also should have led to increased
localization of industry within the manufacturing belt. The
only difference is that instead of an increased share of manufactures per se in demand, the necessary change is an increased share of manufactures that are used as inputs into
other manufactures. But this did of course happen, as the
"industrial ecology" of the U.S. economy became more diverse and complex. So it is not surprising that localization of
industry, the emergence of sharply distinct industrial charac-
ters for particular cities or districts, became a striking charac-
teristic of the American economy by the end of the century.

Technological Spillovers
I have saved for last the reason for localization that many
economists would put first—namely, the more or less pure
externality that results from knowledge spillovers between

nearby firms. The emphasis on high technology in much policy discussion and the fame of such clusters as California's Silicon Valley and Boston's Route 128 have made technological externalities the most obvious thing to mention. Furthermore, economists with a conventional background still have a hankering to preserve perfect competition in their models; purely technological externalities do this.

Yet I have chosen to put pure technological external economies last, not first, for several reasons. First, it is an empirical fact that many of the industries that are highly localized within the United States now or were highly localized in the past are nothing like high technology sectors. Silicon Valley is famous; but equally remarkable concentrations may be found of carpet producers around Dalton, Georgia; of jewelry producers around Providence, Rhode Island; of financial services in New York; and historically, of such industries as shoes in Massachusetts or rubber in Akron. Evidently forces for localization other than those involving high technology are quite strong.

Second, as a matter of principle I think we should try to focus first on the kinds of external economies that can be modeled other than by assumption. Labor pooling or intermediate goods supply are things that in principle one could examine directly and predict given a knowledge of the technology of the industry. And on the other side, the concreteness of these forces places constraints on what we can assume. Knowledge flows, by contrast, are invisible; they leave no paper trail by which they may be measured and tracked, and there is nothing to prevent the theorist from assuming anything about them that she likes. A sociologist might be able to help with survey methods; but I would like to get as far as possible with drab, down-to-earth economic analysis before turning to the other social sciences.

Finally, high technology is fashionable, and I think we are all obliged to make a deliberate effort to fight against fashionable ideas. It is all too easy to fall into a kind of facile "megatrends" style of thought in which the wonders of the new are cited and easy assumptions are made that everything is different now. Of course the world has changed—but it was a pretty remarkable place even before the coming of large-scale integrated circuits, and even high technology industries respond to old-fashioned economic forces.

So while I am sure that true technological spillovers play an important role in the localization of some industries, one should not assume that this is the typical reason—even in the high technology industries themselves.

Some Empirical Evidence

I have alluded to some facts about the degree of localization of industry within the United States. But what sort of facts do we actually have? One kind of evidence, which I regard as very important in spite of its lack of rigor, consists of case studies. Nothing is better at suggesting the kind of model that we ought to use than a collection of examples, particularly with some historical depth, of how particular industries come to be in particular places. And the stories are often entertaining too. Before turning to stories, however, I want to discuss some very preliminary statistical work that I have undertaken.

The objective of this work was to answer two questions. First, how localized is the "typical" U.S. industry? Are familiar examples like that of the auto concentration around Detroit or high technology in Silicon Valley normal, or are they outliers?

Second, what sorts of industry are highly localized? Are localized industries typically high technology sectors (which would lend support to a technological spillover model), or are they more prosaic? Are they industries that use highly skilled labor or more general-purpose workers?

The technique I have tried to get at these questions is to construct "locational Gini coefficients" for as many U.S. manufacturing industries as possible. A locational Gini curve for an industry is constructed as follows. First, for each of the locational units in our sample we calculate both the share of total national manufacturing employment and the share of national employment in the industry. Then we rank the units by the ratio of these two numbers. Finally, we run down the ranking, keeping a cumulative total of both the sum of total employment share and the sum of employment share in the industry.

Suppose, for example, that there were three regions. Region 1 has 20 percent of total manufacturing employment, but 50 percent of employment in the widget industry. Region 2 has 40 percent of total manufacturing employment, and 40 percent of widget employment. Region 3 has the remaining 40 percent of manufacturing employment, and the remaining 10 percent of widget employment. Then the resulting curve would be the one illustrated in figure 2.4. Clearly, the more the geographical distribution of the widget industry matches that of overall manufacturing, the closer this curve will lie to the 45-degree line. So there is an obvious index of localization: the area between the curve and the 45-degree line. An industry that was not localized at all, but simply spread out in proportion to overall employment, would have an index of 0; one that is concentrated almost entirely in a region with small overall employment would have an index close to 0.5.

In implementing these indices, I (or rather my research assistant) used data on U.S. three-digit industries, classified by states. This is only a preliminary step; although it is illuminating, there are a number of problems that blur the results.

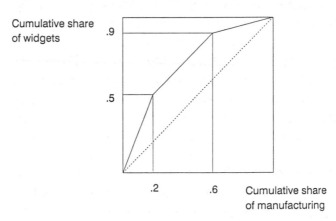

Figure 2.4

First, there are some important holes in the data. The U.S. Bureau of the Census does not reveal information that would compromise the assurance of confidentiality; perhaps surprisingly, this affects data even at the level of large states and big industries. For example, data is withheld on the aircraft industry in Washington (so as not to reveal too much about Boeing) and about the photographic equipment industry in New York (so as to protect Kodak). These are major examples of industry localization, indeed classic ones. Unfortunately, they must simply be dropped from the statistical analysis.

Second, the definition of an industry is problematic. Three-digit industrial classifications are not useless, but they are far from ideal. Old industries, like costume jewelry, rate a three-digit category in spite of very modest employment, while both Silicon Valley and Route 128 are buried inside the huge category of "electronic components." Ideally we would disaggregate and then reaggregate in order to get more meaningful comparisons—but I haven't.

Finally, states aren't really the right geographical units. First of all, they are of very unequal population, which biases industry comparisons: an industry that is completely concentrated around a small town in California will not generate as high a locational Gini as a comparably concentrated industry in Rhode Island. Second, economic regions do not respect state boundaries. The textile complex that shows up very strongly in the data occupies the Piedmont area of the Southeast; state comparisons do not really reveal the compactness (in both the lay and the mathematical senses) of this industry's location.

In spite of all these limitations, we can learn a fair amount from even this preliminary calculation. The results for 106 three-digit industries are reported in appendix D, which also shows total employment in the industry and employment in the three leading states.

The first impression that emerges from the results is that many industries are indeed highly concentrated geographically. The automotive industry offers a useful benchmark. It is a famously localized industry. Although there has been some dispersal since the heyday of Motown, half of the employment is still in the traditional automotive district of southern Michigan and neighboring regions of Indiana and Ohio. So we might expect motor vehicles to be an exceptional industry. But it isn't. It is just slightly above the median. The point is not that automotive production is not highly localized—it is. But so are a lot of other industries.

The other feature of the data that stands out is that the most highly concentrated industries by this admittedly crude calculation are not cutting-edge, high technology sectors. Indeed, the thing that leaps out from the table is not the localization of high technology industries but the cluster of textile-related industries, all of them in more or less the same place: the Piedmont area of the Carolinas and Georgia. Half of the top twenty industries according to my Gini ranking are Piedmont textile sectors. (As we will see in a moment, there is considerable localization of particular industries in this group within the Piedmont; but leave that aside for a moment.)

There is probably a bias in the way this table was constructed against finding the localization of high-tech industries. For one thing, two high-tech industries that are famously geographically localized had to be excluded from the table because of withheld data: aircraft, dominated by Boeing's huge Seattle facilities, and photographic equipment, with Kodak's Rochester complex. These are, of course, industries that are concentrated in ownership as well as in geography.

More important, the fact that the classification scheme is so antiquated means that quite small traditional industries still rate their own three-digit codes, while advanced sectors are buried in meaningless aggregates. Silicon Valley and Route 128 are real enough, but you just can't find them in the statistics.

So I don't want to be misinterpreted. This evidence does not show that high technology industries are not localized. What it shows is simply that low technology industries are also localized. Whatever drives industries to concentrate in one place, it is not solely a matter of technological spillovers.

This is about as far as I want to take this statistical exercise in this lecture; I'll come back to some U.S. regional data in the next lecture. But now I want to get to the fun part and tell stories.

Case Studies: Some Historical Examples
One of the Piedmont textile industries that I found to be highly concentrated geographically was the carpet industry. My

research assistant did some follow-up work on this industry and uncovered a classic case of the role of historical accident and cumulative processes in generating localization. So let's go back to Catherine Evans and her bedspread.

As I mentioned at the beginning of this lecture, in 1895 the teenaged Miss Evans made a bedspread as a gift. The recipients and their neighbors were delighted with the gift, and over the next few years Miss Evans made a number of tufted items, discovering in 1900 a trick of locking the tufts into the backing. She now began to sell the bedspreads, and she and her friends and neighbors launched a local handicraft industry that began selling items well beyond the immediate vicinity.

The handicraft industry became semimechanized in the 1920s, as tufting was used to satisfy the surging demand for chenille sweaters; but production continued to be done by individual households.

Immediately after World War II, however, a machine was developed for producing tufted carpets. Until that time, machine-made carpets had been woven. Tufting proved to be far cheaper. And guess where one could find people who knew about tufting and were quick to see the potential? In the late 1940s and early 1950s, many small carpet firms sprang up in and around Dalton, together with a cluster of supporting firms providing backings, dyeing, etc. Existing carpet manufacturers initially clung to weaving; they eventually either went out of business, driven out by the upstarts from Dalton, or moved their own operations from traditional sites in the Northeast to

Dalton. And so the little Georgia city emerged as America's carpet capital.

It's a lovely story; it's also a very typical one. The whole process of industrialization within the United States was marked by similar stories of small accidents leading to the establishment of one or two persistent centers of production. Anyone who thinks that Silicon Valley is a distinctly modern sort of creation should look at the fascinating monograph, "The Localization of Industries," contained in the 1900 U.S. Census. The monograph identifies fifteen highly localized industries in 1900, including: collars and cuffs, localized in Troy, New York; leather gloves, localized in the two neighboring New York towns of Gloversville (sic) and Johnstown; shoes, in several cities in the northeastern part of Massachusetts; silk goods, in Paterson, New Jersey; jewelry, in and around Providence, Rhode Island; and agricultural machinery, in Chicago.

In each of these cases there is a story similar to, if not quite as charming, as that of Catherine Evans. An accident led to the establishment of the industry in a particular location, and thereafter cumulative processes took over. The Massachusetts shoe industry owed its start to the Welsh cobbler John Adams Dagyr, who set up shop in 1750; the dominance of the Providence jewelry industry (which still makes it onto our list of highly localized industries!) began when a local man invented "filled" gold in 1794; the reign of Troy as the detachable collar and cuff center (alas, fashion!) was inaugurated by a Methodist minister in the 1820s.

What is important to the economist here is, of course, not the initial accident but the nature of the cumulative process that allowed such accidents to have such large and long-lasting effects. What the historical record shows us are two things. First, such cumulative processes are pervasive; Silicon Valley is not at all unique, either in time or space, but is simply a glitzy version of a traditional phenomenon. And second, Marshall's first two reasons for localization, labor pooling and the supply of specialized inputs, play a large role even when pure technological externalities seem unlikely to be important.

Has the basis of localization shifted over time? The authors of the monograph in the twelfth census thought that it would. They noted that many of the highly localized industries were ones that relied heavily on skilled handwork, and speculated that the arbitrary nature of localization would tend to be eroded because "The use of machinery has ... tended to lessen the importance of a specially skilled labor supply. In proportion as an industry becomes automatic, its localization becomes independent of its supply of special labor."

To some extent they were right. First, it is doubtless true that each manufacturing industry, as it matures, tends to become less dependent on the pooled labor market, specialized inputs, and information spillovers that sustain localization. Consider, for example, the U.S. tire industry. Before 1930 this industry was spectacularly localized in the city of Akron, to which financial incentives from the chamber of commerce (industrial policy!) had lured one Benjamin Franklin Goodrich. As Detroit boomed, the rubber center in Akron came to have more than a hundred firms, generating some of the highest wages in the United States and attracting migrants from all over (including my grandfather). Time was not, however, on Akron's side. As tire production became standardized, it could be delocalized and moved closer to the market. The market itself spread out over time as the auto industry began to establish assembly plants around the United States.

As it turned out, the end was rather sudden. The Depression dealt a devastating blow to Akron's economy and apparently destroyed the critical mass of rubber firms there: when the country emerged, the role of Akron as a rubber center was gone. No major producers of tires are now located in the one-time tire capital of the world.

But while the Akron story shows that localization within an industry tends to fade away, there are always new industries. Detroit fades, but Silicon Valley rises. Indeed, surely there is a kind of product cycle, in which emergent new industries initially flourish in localized industrial districts, then disperse as they mature.

High Technology Clusters

In the last generation, the familiar examples of localization have changed. One rarely now hears about Motown, or Iron City, or the garment district (although they still exist in some-what attenuated form). Instead it is all high tech: Silicon Valley, Route 128, Research Triangle. How do these new clusters compare with the older localization?

The first thing to say is that on the whole the stories of their founding are less romantic. In general the new high technology clusters were the product less of intrepid individuals than of visionary bureaucrats (if that is not an oxymoron). But otherwise the stories look rather similar.

Silicon Valley was created largely through the initiative of Fred Terman, the vice-president of Stanford University. Through his initiative the university provided an initial stake for Hewlett-Packard, which became the nucleus of the Valley. It also established the famous research park on university land, on which first Hewlett-Packard, then many other firms, began operations. There was a noticeable cumulative process operating through the university itself: the revenues from the research park helped to finance Stanford's ascent to world-class status in science and engineering, and the university's rise helped make Silicon Valley an attractive place for high-tech business.

Route 128 was created, in a more diffuse way, through the initiative of MIT's president, Karl Compton, who encouraged MIT faculty to become entrepreneurs and helped mobilize private venture capital.

North Carolina's Research Triangle, finally, was created through state support of a research park, in direct emulation of Silicon Valley and Route 128.

Perhaps the most important thing to emphasize in these high technology stories is the importance of non-high-technology factors in the agglomerative process. Both in Silicon Valley and around Route 128 a key advantage is the existence of a pool of people with certain skills. In the Boston area, for example, growth companies in the software field can be reasonably sure of being able to find people with esoteric knowledge in a variety of sub-subdisciplines. At the same time, the Boston area has been a good place for people to invest in acquiring these skills, or for those with those skills to live: if a start-up goes bust, as many do, you can find another job without having to relocate. This is just the labor pooling story; the fact that the skill involves high technology, rather than shoemaking or tufting, may be of secondary importance.

An anecdote: when involved with the MIT productivity commission, which eventually produced the best-selling book *Made in America*, I became very unpopular with the engineers for suggesting that some very non-technological-seeming sectors were in economic terms not so different from high tech. For example, consider Milan's fashion industry: a cluster of firms that rely on a highly specialized labor force (designers, models, stitchers, etc.), on specialized suppliers (fabrics, dyes, makeup, etc.), and on early access to information (what's in, what's out). I argued that economically Milan and Route 128 are similar creatures. The engineers thought I was frivolous.

Services

In the late twentieth century the great bulk of our labor force makes services rather than goods. Many of these services are nontradable and simply follow the geographical distribution of the goods-producing population—fast-food outlets, daycare providers, divorce lawyers surely have locational Ginis pretty close to zero. Some services, however, especially in the financial sector, can be traded. Hartford is an insurance city; Chicago the center of futures trading; Los Angeles the entertainment capital; and so on.

The most spectacular examples of localization in today's world are, in fact, based on services rather than manufacturing. Tokyo and London are not essentially manufacturers. Even Silicon Valley and Route 128 are in effect more nearly centers that supply services to manufacturing than actual physical production sites. And arguably technology is moving in a direction that will promote more localization of services. Transportation of goods has not gotten much cheaper in the past eighty years: the epochal innovations were railroads and steamboats, with everything since representing only modest improvements. But the ability to transmit *information* has grown spectacularly, with telecommunication, computers, fiber optics, etc.

Some trends are visible. One of my students has been looking at the data on the growing concentration of wealth in Southeastern England; he finds that it is the service industries that are concentrating there, while manufacturing is actually shifting the other way.

The important point is that the logic of localization remains similar. Catherine Evanses—that is, small accidental events—start a cumulative process in which the presence of a large number of firms and workers acts as an incentive for still more firms and workers to congregate at a particular location. The resulting pattern may be determined by underlying resources and technology at some very aggregative level; but at ground level there is a striking role for history and accident.

This lecture is being given a few miles from Brussels, the headquarters of the European Commission. Let me be a little silly and describe the commission's mission as being to do at a practical level what I am trying to do at an intellectual level: to eliminate international economics (within Europe) and replace it with economic geography. If 1992 does what it is supposed to, then eventually the EC will constitute as integrated an economic area as the United States.

What difference will that make—and is it a good thing? More generally, where does the nation-state fit into the story of economic geography as I have been telling it? In the first lecture I suggested the usefulness of taking nations out of the story of interregional trade; now I have to try to put them back in.

In doing this, I want reverse the order of the previous lectures. In those lectures I started with economic geography at the grand level of regional development, of center versus periphery, largely because I had a cleaner model; only then did I turn to the more modest issue of industry localization. Today I want to start more modestly, then move up to the big story.

Before I can do either, however, we need to spend a little time on the question of what a nation is, on how we should think about the role of political boundaries in economic geography.

What Is a Nation?

Let me start by emphasizing what a nation is *not*. A nation is not a region or a single location. That is, when we talk about the external economies that I have argued drive both localization and the emergence of core-periphery patterns, there is no reason to suppose that political boundaries define the relevant unit over which those external economies apply.

Suppose, for example, that I am interested in the economies of localization. These arise, I argued, from the standard Marshallian trinity of labor market pooling, supply of intermediate goods, and knowledge spillovers. All three of these probably typically arise at the level of a single city or small cluster of cities, an area small enough to make it possible for people to change jobs without changing houses, for hard-to-transport goods and services to be delivered, and for regular personal contact to take place. There is no reason to think that Vancouver and Montreal generate much in the way of joint localization economies—and certainly no reason to think that the spillovers between them are more important than those between Vancouver and Seattle.

Suppose, on the other hand, that I am interested in the grand agglomerative tendencies of the core-periphery model. Here the nature of the externality, I have argued, comes from market size effects in the face of transportation costs—from the forward and backward linkages that make producers want to concentrate near large markets—and puts large markets where producers concentrate. And here again there is no particular reason to think that national boundaries define a relevant region. To stay with my U.S.-Canadian example, surely Toronto is part of the core—indeed, industrial Ontario is generally considered by geographers to be part of a common American manufacturing belt—while Idaho is part of the periphery. The traditional European manufacturing belt sprawled across the boundaries of France, Belgium, Luxembourg, and Germany, but did not include the city in which this lecture is being given.

All this may seem pretty obvious, but economists still often get it wrong. Only a few years ago it was common for economic analyses of increasing returns and trade to assume that external economies applied at the level of a nation and to assert as their main result that big countries tend to export goods characterized by economies of scale. The result may still be true—but it will be true because national policies make it so, not because there is anything of inherent economic importance in drawing a line on the ground and calling the land on either side two different countries.

All of which leads us to the real reason why national boundaries matter and to the proper notion of a nation for our analysis. Nations matter—they exist in a modeling sense—because they have governments whose policies affect the movements of goods and factors. In particular, national boundaries often act as barriers to trade and factor mobility. Every modern nation has restrictions on labor mobility. Many nations place restrictions on the movement of capital, or at least threaten to do so. And actual or potential limits on trade are pervasive, in spite of the best efforts of trade negotiators.

The force of these limits varies. In the era during which the U.S. manufacturing belt was emerging, European nations were delinking their economies through tariffs (and eventually war). Trade in manufactured goods among advanced countries is at this point fairly free, and in principle entirely free within the EC—although as we will see shortly, the extent of industry localization within the EC remains considerably less than within the United States. Labor mobility, by contrast, is far less today than in the era before World War I. Indeed, in the great era of European emigration, when migrants had to choose among Canada, Argentina, Australia, and the United States, we may suggest that at the margin effective labor mobility among these countries was nearly perfect.

But in any case the point is that countries should be defined by their restrictions. With that in mind, let us turn to the role of nations in industry localization.

Localization and Trade

Samuelson's Angel
If trade were completely free, the immobility of labor and even of capital among nation-states would not necessarily pose a

barrier to industry localization. Instead, each country would tend to develop its own set of localized industries, exporting the products of those industries it has, importing those it does not.

A useful way to think about this is via a fable. This fable was initially suggested by Paul Samuelson to explain the essence of the Heckscher-Ohlin model, but Elhanan Helpman and I have applied it extensively to trade in the presence of increasing returns.

Once upon a time, Samuelson supposed, there was an economy that was in equilibrium. (Strange how quickly the romance of the fable fades!) Capital and labor worked together freely, producing capital-intensive and labor-intensive goods alike. But the factors of production grew arrogant, daring to challenge heaven, and an angel descended and divided them into nations. Capital from one nation could henceforth work only with labor from that same nation—and the angel did not divide the capital and labor equally. What were the chastened factors of production to do?

The answer, of course, is that if the angel did not divide the factors of production too unequally, it would still be possible through trade to "reproduce the integrated economy." Nations that had a high ratio of capital to labor could concentrate on producing and exporting capital-intensive goods, trading them for labor-intensive goods from other nations, and achieve the same overall production and factor returns as before the angel's descent. Trade in goods would essentially be an indirect way of achieving the now-forbidden trade in factors of production.

It is immediately obvious that this fable can be extended to encompass localization as well as comparative advantage. Suppose that before the angel's descent there were certain goods whose production was localized in particular industrial districts. After the angel's descent it may still be possible to achieve the same result: if no one district uses too much capital and labor, it will be possible for each industrial district to "fit" inside one of the new national economies, exporting its products while buying the products of other industrial districts in other countries.

Trade, in this extended fable, will arise from a mix of motives. It will represent both an indirect way to trade factors of production and a way to achieve the economies of localization. It will also ordinarily be beneficial to all concerned. Provided that the angel was not too malicious—carving up the world into countries too small to accommodate industrial districts or too unequally endowed with capital and labor to make up for their deficiencies through trade—everyone will achieve the same returns that she would have in the integrated economy. And trade will be beneficial both because of the gains from implicit trade in factors and because of the ability to realize the gains from localization.

This is a fairly pleasant story. How well does it correspond to what actually happens, and is its benign implication really right?

Europe versus America

Here as in the first lecture I have tried some first-pass quantification in an effort to get some empirical feel for the issues. Again the approach is crude but suggestive; because I now need to deal with international data, the results are even cruder. But they are, I think, interesting.

The starting point of this piece of work is the observation that the "great regions" of the United States—the Northeast (New England plus Middle Atlantic), the Midwest (East North Central and West North Central), the South, and the West— are comparable in population and economic size to the European Big Four. So one might expect that the degree of economic differentiation among U.S. regions and that among European nations might be roughly similar. In fact, one might expect localization to have proceeded further in Europe, if only because the distances involved in the United States are so much greater.

To make the comparison, one needs comparable data. This is a problem. The best I have been able to come up with is a set of employment statistics by (more or less) two-digit industries for European nations, which can be compared with regional employment statistics for (more or less) the same industries for U.S. regions. It's a crude comparison, but the best that I could do.

Using this data, I construct indices of regional/national divergence. These are constructed as follows. Let s_i be the share of industry i in total manufacturing employment in some region/country; and let a "star" indicate that we are referring to some other region/country. Then the index I use is

$$\sum_i \left| s_i - s_i^* \right|.$$

Suppose that two regions had identical industrial structures, that is, that industry shares of employment were the same for all i. Then the index would of course be zero. A little less obviously, if two regions had completely disjoint industry structures, the index would be 2 (because each share in each region would be counted in full). So the index is a rough way of quantifying differences in structures and hence regional specialization.

What I have done is to calculate this index for twelve pairs of regions/nations: for U.S. regions compared with one another, and for Europe's Big Four compared with one another. (I don't trust the comparability of the data enough to try the direct U.S.-Europe indices.) The results are shown in table 3.1.

The result does not come through as strongly as I would have liked, probably because the data are grossly overaggregated, but it is there: European nations are less specialized than U.S. regions. You might have the impression that the United States is a great homogeneous society in which regional differences have faded away, and culturally you would be right. But in terms of the economic roles they play, U.S. regions are more distinct than European nations.

A somewhat clearer picture emerges if I cheat a little and focus on what I think is the most revealing case. Compare the

Table 3.1
Indices of industrial specialization

A. U.S. regions, 1977	NE	MW	S	W
NE	-	.224	.247	.242
MW	-	-	.336	.182
S	-	-	-	.271

B. EC countries, 1985	FR	FRG	IT	UK
FR	-	.200	.197	.083
FRG	-	-	.175	.184
IT	-	-	-	.184

specializations of the Midwest and the South, on one hand, and of Germany and Italy, on the other. In both cases we are in effect comparing a traditional heavy industrial producer with a traditional light, labor-intensive producer. And as we see in table 3.2, which compares employment shares in selected sectors, the patterns of revealed comparative advantage in key industries are similar.

But the degree of specialization in accord with this revealed comparative advantage is very different. At one extreme, the Midwest has essentially no textile industry, compared with Germany's still substantial one. At the other, the South produces far less machinery than Italy.

Let me offer another illustrative comparison, this one of the automotive industry. Table 3.3 compares the regional distribution of the U.S. auto industry with the national distribution of the European industry. What it shows is that the U.S.

Table 3.2
Industrial specialization (share of manufacturing employment)

	Germany	Italy	Midwest	South
Textiles	3.7	9.1	0.3	11.7
Apparel	2.6	5.6	2.4	10.6
Machinery	15.8	12.9	15.0	7.1
Transportation equipment	13.2	10.4	12.8	5.9
Sum of share differences	35.2		62.6	

Table 3.3
Distribution of auto production (percentages)

U.S.		EC	
Midwest	66.3	Germany	38.5
South	25.4	France	31.1
West	5.1	Italy	17.6
Northeast	3.2	U.K.	12.9

industry is far more localized. In essence, the U.S. industry is a Midwestern phenomenon, with only a scattering of assembly plants in other parts of the country. The European equivalent would be a concentration of half the industry within 150 kilometers of Wolfsburg.

So although the data are spotty, the conclusion seems clear: localization has gone much further in America than in Europe.

Why? Obviously the reason is the existence of barriers to trade. I find it helpful to return to one of the localization stories from the last lecture, the one that focused on intermediate goods.

There I pointed out that there is a strong analogy between the core-periphery model and a simplified model in which each manufactured good within an industry is both a final and an intermediate good. In both cases concentration tends to take place when transportation costs fall and economies of scale increase. (The difference is that the share of manufacturing in demand in the core-periphery model corresponds, in the case of the intermediate goods model, to the share of output that is used as an input.)

Consider what happened during the nineteenth century: in both Europe and America, transportation costs fell and economies of scale grew more important. Thus the logic of localization grew stronger. But in Europe the fall of transport costs was opposed by tariffs, often rising ones. And of course for forty-five years after 1913, Europe was fragmented by exchange controls and, alas, worse things. Even since the formation of the EC, borders have remained significant nuisance barriers to trade, supplemented by differences in regulation and more subtle government policies that discriminate in favor of national products. The result is that European economic localization has remained far short of U.S. levels.

This comparison has a number of interesting implications for the future of the European economy, as it becomes more integrated. Let me focus on two: the potential adjustment problems and the issue of monetary union.

Suppose that eventually Europe will look like America, with a similar degree of localization and specialization. On the road from here to there, this will have to mean a process of unraveling of at least some European industrial centers. If table 3.2 is any guide, Germany in an integrated European economy should be set to experience an unraveling of its textile and apparel industries and a relocation of those industries to Southern Europe, comparable to the relocation of traditional New England industries to the Southeastern United States in the early twentieth century. Offsetting this should be the rise of German industrial clusters in key heavy and high technology industries, while such industries in Southern Europe contract—which could be seen as a kind of Mezzogiornification of the South, even if it is in fact beneficial to both sides.

Now one can make a case that this process of specialization will, in manufacturing at least, be less dramatic than the U.S. comparison suggests. For one thing, there may be multiple equilibria that differ in the degree of localization as well as the specific choice of location. That is, if the United States had happened to develop two auto centers instead of one, it is possible that both would have survived; and the relatively dispersed European geography of manufacturing may survive better than a direct comparison with the United States would suggest. (I'll offer a clearer version of this argument when we come to center-periphery issues a little later.) Also, within the United States the trend over time has actually been toward delocalization of manufactures. Table 3.4 compares those indices of regional differentiation in 1947 and in 1985: there has been a definite decline. That is, the high-water mark of manufacturing localization in the United States was reached a long time ago, probably in the 1920s. If we think of Europe as

Table 3.4
Indices of U.S. regional specialization

A. 1947	MW	NE	S	W
MW	-	.361	.606	.441
NE	-	-	.560	.504
S	-	-	-	.403

B. 1985	MW	NE	S	W
MW	-	.224	.336	.182
NE	-	-	.247	.242
S	-	-	-	.271

converging to where the United States will be, not where it now is, the extent of adjustment required looks a lot smaller.

On the other hand, services are probably becoming more concentrated in the United States. If Europe were to follow suit, we would have virtually all sophisticated financial activity carried out in London; the whole entertainment industry in, say, Madrid; most sophisticated software designed near Oxford; all insurance companies headquartered in . . . well, you get the idea.

The point, in any case, is that 1992 may not look like 1958. In the first great movement toward European economic integration, virtually all of the increase in trade took the form of "intra-industry" rather than "inter-industry" trade and brought relatively few problems of industrial adjustment. This time, as true U.S.-style industrial specialization takes hold, the transition may not be so easy to live through.

Going beyond the transition, what about monetary union? I have had nothing to say about money or exchange rates in these lectures so far, and I do not intend to say much here. The economic geography approach does, however, suggest that some commonly held conceptions need to be questioned. In particular, it has become near orthodoxy in Europe that 1992 paves the way for EMU—that closer economic integration makes the gains from monetary union greater, and the costs less.

This reasoning is based in part on the standard optimum currency area argument. We hypothesize that monetary union brings both benefits (reduced transaction costs in international trade, greater credibility and stability of monetary policy) and costs (greater difficulty in adjusting to country-specific shocks). The usual argument is that the greater the trade between two nations, the larger the gains from a common currency and the less the value of the freedom to adjust exchange rates. Because 1992 will lead to increased trade, it strengthens the case for a common currency.

So far so good. But it is also the case that the costs of a common currency are less the more similar two countries are in their output mix (and thus the less idiosyncratic the shocks they face). The general presumption among European analysts has been that 1992 will be accompanied by and indeed facilitate a continuing convergence of economic structure among EC nations, so that the case for a common currency derives yet a further impetus.

But if the evidence presented in the last few tables is right, European nations are likely to become less similar, not more, as a result of 1992—and they will in this respect become less suitable as an optimum currency area as a result of increased integration. (A side implication, of course, is that the United States is arguably less suitable for a single currency than Europe!)

I don't want to push this any further; let it stand as a surprise question raised by the geographical approach to international economics.

Center and Periphery, Again

We now turn from the specialization of economies to their size. I argued in lecture 1 that the interaction of increasing returns and transportation costs can explain uneven regional development at a grand level, with regions that have a head start in production attracting industry away from those with less favorable initial conditions.

This observation immediately raises a number of questions about competition among nations. Should small countries fear economic integration, lest their industry be pulled into the inevitably larger cores of their larger neighbors? Should countries pursue deliberate policies to ensure that they get their industrial cores? Does the core-periphery model explain uneven development at a national as well as a regional level?

Let's take a rough look at these questions.

Who Gets the Core?

At first sight, the two-region model developed in lecture 1 seems to have ominous implications for small countries. Shouldn't we think of two countries as two regions, with the larger country having the larger initial population—and thus, probably, attracting all industry away from the smaller nation?

Well, not necessarily—because countries are not identical to regions. To take the most spectacular recent example, we have suddenly become aware that the Soviet Union, although a huge economic unit, is a collection of regional economies; if, as seems to be happening, that economy breaks up into its geographical components, those components will individually bulk no larger than the nation's erstwhile Eastern European satellites.

So it may be more accurate to think of a large country as consisting of many regions, not big regions. And once we think of countries as collections of regions, we discover that it is by no means necessarily true that economic integration will favor regions in the larger country.

To see why, we need to be able to think about the core-periphery model in a multiregional framework, to get away from the two-region model. In the grand tradition of location theory, of course, we would go the whole way by abandoning the notion of regions altogether, imagining a continuous distribution of population across a two-dimensional plane. But that is much harder than anything I want to tackle right now. Let me instead assume a discrete set of regions, laid out in a one-dimensional space; because I don't want to worry about end points, this space will have to be a circle. And I want to have as few regions as possible, consistent with telling some interesting stories; this turns out to be six. The resulting story is illustrated in figures 3.1 and 3.2: six regions laid out in a circle, with transportation possible only around the circle (impassable mountains in the middle).

As in lecture 1, imagine that there are two kinds of people: farmers, who are spread equally among the regions, and workers, who can choose where to live. Then one possibility is that the economy will form a single core; this is suggested in figure 3.1 by the shading of one region. Alternatively, if transport costs are high, economies of scale weak, and the share of "footloose" production small, manufacturing production may be spread evenly across the regions.

But there is another possibility, which is that the economy may support multiple cores. A particularly plausible example is

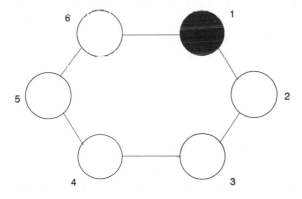

Figure 3.1

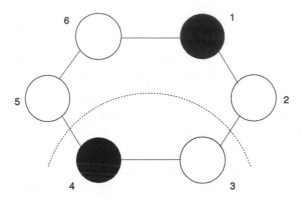

Figure 3.2

illustrated in figure 3.2, in which the shading indicates the formation of two cores at regions 1 and 4. Each core will have a "hinterland" consisting of the two neighboring regions.

Which of these pictures is right? The answer presumably depends on the same parameters that, as we saw in lecture 1, determine whether a core-periphery pattern emerges in the two-region case. If transport costs are low, economies of scale large, and the share of footloose industry in national income large, the result will be a single core; if the reverse is true, there may be no core at all; intermediate levels will support a multiple-core structure.[1]

Now consider the following hypothetical history: Initially the world illustrated in figures 3.1 and 3.2 consists of two separate countries, one of four regions, one of two; the boundary is

---

1. As the analysis of lecture 1 also suggested, there may be more than one equilibrium structure—that is, both one-core and two-core geographies might be possible even for a given set of tastes and technology. Consider this point registered, then ignored, for the discussion that follows.

illustrated by the dotted line in figure 3.2. And we suppose that the two countries initially maintain sufficient barriers to trade and factor mobility that their economic geography evolves independently, with the large country developing a core in region 1 and the small country a smaller core in region 2. Then the two countries do a 1992, and merge into a single economic unit. What happens?

The answer depends on whether the ultimate equilibrium has one core or two. If the integrated economy ends up with only one core, then region 1, with its head start, will presumably attract all the manufacturing away from region 4. But if the integrated economy ends up with two cores, manufacturing in region 4 will actually expand at the expense of region 1, as it gains access to its full natural hinterland.

There is, I suppose, some presumption that the larger country will tend to gain manufacturing at the expense of the smaller when they integrate, because it is more likely to have large cores. But it is only a presumption, not a certainty—and the point is that one needs to think about the geographical structure of production, not treat countries as natural units of analysis.

Fighting for the Core?

We have seen that the two-region model, in which there can be only one core, can be misleading for international issues. Nonetheless, let us return to the two-region setup to ask a rather different question: does the geographical viewpoint have any implications for policy?

Now any model with mobile factors raises a basic question for policy analysis: on whose behalf should policy be made? Should Germany's social welfare function include *gastar-beiter* who happen to work there, but whose roots are in Turkey; should Turkey's include people who have moved to Germany?

Let me cheat and adopt a clearly inadequate concept: that of measuring the welfare of the immobile factors only. This amounts to taking into account only the "farmers" in our core-periphery model, while ignoring the "workers." For serious policy analysis it clearly won't do; but all I want to do is to make a point: that there may well be an incentive for countries to try to use trade protection and/or other policies to make sure that they get the core, or at least prevent their nascent core from being pulled away by neighbors.

It may be useful once again to present a suggestive picture (figure 3.3). In this picture I envision a two-region world of the kind described in lecture 1. What the picture shows is the welfare of the immobile "farmers" in each region as a function of the level of transport cost. When transport costs are high, there will not be a core-periphery pattern, so if the regions are of equal size, their farmers will have the same level of welfare. Lowering transport costs will raise welfare in each, to at least some extent, simply by increasing interregional trade.

If transport costs fall enough, however, we will reach the critical point at which the regions become differentiated into a manufacturing core and an agricultural periphery. And when that threshold is crossed, it is apparent that whereas immobile factors in the region that becomes the core will gain,

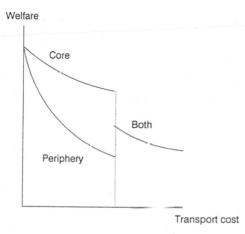

Figure 3.3

initially those in the other region will lose (because they will now have to import all their manufactures).

If transport costs were to fall still further, welfare would again rise in both regions. It would also converge: as transport costs go to zero, location ceases to matter, and both regions reach a common level of welfare that is higher than they would have had at high transport costs. This immediately suggests that for the region that becomes the periphery, there is a U-shaped relationship between economic integration and welfare: close integration is good, but a limited move toward integration may hurt, a point that I will return to shortly. For now, however, let me focus on what happens near the critical level of transport costs at which the regions become differentiated.

What is clear is that (1) the immobile factors in a region would prefer to be in the core rather than the periphery, and (2) modest policy actions at the critical point can tip the balance in one region's favor. Imagine that it is 1860, and you perceive correctly that the invention of railroads is about to lead to the division of your continent into a manufacturing nation that contains a core and an agricultural nation that does not. Then you might very plausibly advocate a temporary tariff to ensure that you get the core. Once you have established a decisive lead in manufacturing, you can remove the tariff— and lecture the other country, which has effectively become your economic colony, on the virtues of free trade.

Has anything like this ever happened? Well, not exactly. But there is a story with some of the basic elements, and in which I think it is possible to make a pretty good defense of protectionism: the case of Canada before World War I.

Canadian Economic Nationalism

In 1873, when the various British colonies north of the United States were gathered under a single government, it looked likely that the whole nation would become part of the North American periphery to the already coalescing U.S. manufacturing belt.[2] We are used to thinking of Canada, like the United States, as being a great immigrant nation. In its early years as a nation, however, Canada attracted few immigrants from abroad—and Canadians, especially from impoverished Quebec, were migrating in substantial numbers to the United States. There was little manufacturing in Canada and seemingly little prospect that any would arise. Agricultural expan-

---

2. This section is based on Buckberg 1990.

sion was proceeding westward into the prairies, much as it was in the United States, but as in the United States it was not pulling manufacturing and urbanization west with it.

If one had made a guess in 1870, one would probably have predicted an agricultural Canada of perhaps 5 or at most 10 million people—a sort of oversized Nebraska. Most of those people would have been fairly prosperous, much as most U.S. farmers are; but there wouldn't have been much of a nation.

What happened instead, of course, was a deliberate policy of delinking from the U.S. economy. In 1878 Canada introduced the so-called National Policy, which had two main elements: a tariff wall that in effect forced the Canadian agricultural sector to turn to domestic producers rather than established U.S. suppliers, and a national railway that in effect subsidized East-West traffic in opposition to the natural North-South direction.

Isn't this simply a standard kind of infant-industry, import-substitution policy, of the kind that has gotten such a bad name in the past forty years? Not quite. Until the 1920s, Canada and the United States were in a fairly unusual situation with respect to one another: in effect labor mobility between the two was nearly perfect. The reason is that both countries were the targets of large-scale, economically motivated immigration, and so on the margin were competing for workers.

But what that means is that Canadian import substitution could do something that similar policies elsewhere cannot: by protecting the domestic market, they could also enlarge it. Because Canadian farmers were forced to buy Canadian, there were more Canadians than there would otherwise have been and hence a larger Canadian market. In principle, that market would eventually be large enough to be self-sustaining. That is, the Canadian market would eventually become large enough to make it efficient to locate manufacturing there to serve the market even without protection. At that point the economy could throw away its crutches and accept free trade without fear of becoming peripheralized. This is not so much an infant-industry as an infant-country argument for protection.

Was this policy a success? Presumably that depends on one's objectives. What seems clear is that the policy did more than create a hothouse industrial sector that would die off as soon as it was exposed to the winds of international competition. Canada now is strong enough industrially to accept free trade with the United States without fearing that it will be peripheralized. (Well, okay, some Canadians still fear it, and they could even be right; but they are a minority and are probably wrong.) It seems reasonable to argue that Canada's nationalistic economic policies were the key factor in creating this strength.

Geography and the European Periphery

At the start of this lecture I suggested that the economics of Europe are in the process of ceasing to be international and becoming interregional instead. If this means increased localization of industries, it will pose some problems of adjustment, presumably offset by increased efficiency. But what if it turns out that an integrated Europe gravitates toward a geography in which everything footloose clusters in the northwest corner of the continent, at the expense of outlying regions? Can the European idea survive?

Let me start with some facts about Europe at present, then ask what may happen in the future.

Center and Periphery in Europe Today

The population distribution of Europe does not at present exhibit anything like the unevenness of the American distribution. Within countries there are some core-periphery patterns: the continuing pull of greater London or of the Ile-de-France look familiar to Americans (and the landscape around these centers looks increasingly indistinguishable from my beloved, picturesque Northeastern Corridor). But in spite of considerable migration from South to North in the 1960s and early 1970s, there has been no wholesale concentration of population and employment in the areas of early industrialization. The reason is obvious: Europe has historically been far less integrated, both in terms of factor mobility and in terms of trade, than the United States.

On the other hand, Europe is characterized by a very strong center-periphery pattern when one considers not population but purchasing power. Interregional income differentials within Europe are much larger than within the United States, and they are closely associated with geographical position. The European Commission has constructed an index of peripherality based on the distance of regions from markets and has classified regions according to this index; as table 3.5 shows, there is a remarkably strong gradient in income.

To a certain school of thought—say to Immanuel Wallerstein or Nicholas Kaldor—table 3.5 would look like a causal relationship running from peripherality to income. It is not hard to develop a variant of the core-periphery model that does not need factor mobility to function. Suppose that through forward and backward linkages, a region that has accumulated a lot of physical and human capital tends to have a higher, rather than a lower, rate of return on investment than a region where these factors are scarce. And suppose that the rate of capital accumulation itself depends on the rate of return. Then one can imagine an unequalizing spiral in which the world endogenously becomes differentiated into rich and poor nations. This story makes sense, especially given the kind of models that I have been examining; and it is indeed a story that I have written up elsewhere (Krugman 1981).

Table 3.5
Peripherality and per capita GNP in Europe

	(EC average = 100)
Central	122
Intermediate	105
Inner periphery	89
Outer periphery	64

Although there is surely some causation running from peripherality to low income in Europe, however, I would guess pretty strongly that the main causation runs the other way. That is, northwestern Europe is relatively rich for reasons that have to do more with culture than with geography.[3] And as a result, the richer regions are also relatively close to the large markets, which are themselves.

So I would guess that Europe's center-periphery pattern is not primarily the result of the kinds of forces that I have stressed in these lectures—though I am willing to be proved wrong. Nonetheless, that center-periphery pattern is there: that is, the poorer regions of Europe are in general also relatively distant from markets.[4]

What will happen to these regions as Europe become more closely integrated? The general presumption has been that with improved access of low-wage regions to the advanced European core, manufacturing will want to shift out to the periphery. This may be how it will work out. But Tony Venables and I (Krugman and Venables 1990) have argued that this presumption isn't necessarily right: improved access might actually hurt, not help, peripheral industry.

---

3. As Robert Solow once remarked, efforts to explain differences in national income levels and growth rates usually end in a "blaze of amateur sociology."
4. When I was a child, I distinctly remember seeing a set of "science facts" that included this rather Zen-like observation: "Although the moon is smaller than the Earth, it is also farther away."

Integration and Peripheral Industry

Imagine an industry that can locate in one or both of two places: a "central" nation in which the wage rate and hence production costs are high but which has good access to markets; or a "peripheral" nation in which labor costs are low but access to markets is less good. You might imagine that a reduction in transportation costs would always tend to shift production away from the center to the periphery; but you would be wrong.

The reason is that reducing transportation costs has two effects: it facilitates locating production where it is cheapest, but it also facilitates concentration of production in one location, so as to realize economies of scale. And when production is concentrated, it may pay to concentrate it at the location with higher costs but better access.

Table 3.6 offers a hypothetical example, initially suggested by Venables and myself. We imagine a good that can be produced in either or both of two locations: "Belgium," which we take to be a central nation, and "Spain," which we take to lie on the periphery. For simplicity, we imagine that total sales may be

Table 3.6
Hypothetical effects of lower trade barriers

		Shipping costs		
	Production costs	High	Medium	Low
Produce in Belgium	10	3	1.5	0
Produce in Spain	8	8	4	0
Produce in both	12	0	0	0

taken as given, that is, ignore any elasticity of demand and simply suppose that the location of production is chosen so as to minimize the sum of production and transportation costs. It is cheaper to produce the good in Spain than in Belgium, because Spanish wages are lower; but it is cheaper to produce the good in either location than in both, because of economies of scale. On the other hand, producing in both locations minimizes transport costs, while producing in central Belgium involves lower transport costs than producing on the periphery.

In table 3.6 we show three cases: high, intermediate, and low (in fact zero) transport costs. Not too surprisingly, if transport costs are high production will take place in both countries, whereas if they are low, it will take place in low-wage Spain. But a reduction of transport costs—in table 3.6, a 50 percent reduction in costs from the "high" case—actually causes the location of production to shift away from low-cost Spain to high-cost Belgium.

The reason is that in the medium transport cost case, costs are low enough to make it worthwhile to concentrate production, but still high enough that access to markets outweighs production cost as a determinant of location. So the relationship between transport costs and Spanish output in this industry is U-shaped rather than monotonic: over some range closer integration actually leads production to move perversely from the point of view of comparative cost.

Again, at a guess I would suppose that we are now on the good part of the U, not the bad: that railroads and steamships led to deindustrialization of the periphery, but that 1992 will actually favor peripheral manufacturing. But we cannot be sure—and service industries, whose products are still difficult to transport, may recapitulate the history of manufactures.

Concluding Thoughts

There are costs to transactions across space; there are economies of scale in production. These two facts are the key to the story told in these lectures. Because of economies of scale, producers have an incentive to concentrate production of each good or service in a limited number of locations. Because of the costs of transacting across distance, the preferred locations for each individual producer are those where demand is large or supply of inputs is particularly convenient—which in general are the locations chosen by other producers. Thus concentrations of industry, once established, tend to be self-sustaining; this applies both to the localization of individual industries and to such grand agglomerations as the Boston-Washington corridor.

I explained this basic idea to a non-economist friend, who replied in some dismay, "Isn't that pretty obvious?" And of course it is. It was obvious to Alfred Marshall, to Allyn Young, to Gunnar Myrdal, to Albert Hirschman, to Allan Pred, and to Nicholas Kaldor. There is a sense in which these lectures are only a repetition of familiar ideas.

Yet while the ideas may be familiar, they have never become part of the mainstream of economic analysis. In the first lecture

I suggested that the main reason for this was the inability of economists to produce models of economic geography that satisfied the profession's ever-growing demand for rigor; and that this inability was in turn essentially tied to the problem of modeling market structure. In this sense these lectures are different from what came before: thanks to the efforts of industrial organization and trade theorists over the past twenty years, it is now possible to do geography as rigorously as you like. The geographers themselves probably won't like this: the economics profession's simultaneous love of rigor and contempt for realism will surely prove infuriating. I do not come here, however, to fight against the sociology of my profession, but to exploit it: by demonstrating that models of economic geography can be cute and fun, I hope to attract other people into tilling this nearly virgin soil.

The rewards will, I hope, be substantial. Regional comparisons offer a huge, almost untapped source of evidence about how our economy really works. In these lectures I have offered a few quick-and-dirty calculations based on casual use of readily available data; surely much more can be accomplished by someone with the patience for real empirical work.

Economic geography is also of considerable policy relevance. Regional issues are important in and of themselves; I have tried in this third lecture to suggest that a geographic perspective is also useful in offering an alternative approach to international economic issues.

Most important to my mind, however, is the support that the study of economic geography offers for a basic rethinking of economics. In spite of a growing interest in "path dependence," most economic analysis remains dominated by a style of model that I like to think of as TTFE: the idea that the economy's behavior is basically determined by its (exogenously given) tastes, technology, and factor endowments. In opposition to TTFE is what Paul David (1985) calls QWERTY (after the arbitrary layout of the typewriter keyboard): the idea that important aspects of an economy are contingent, determined by history and accident.

Many economists find QWERTY deeply disturbing and troubling. Like Paul David, Brian Arthur (1986, 1990), and others before them, I find it exciting and inspiring. But what I conclude even from this preliminary study of economic geography is that it doesn't matter whether you find path dependence appealing or appalling. For at least insofar as the location of economic activity in space is concerned, the idea that an economy's form is largely shaped by historical contingency is not a metaphysical hypothesis; it is simply the obvious truth.

Appendix A:

The Core-Periphery Model

Lecture 1 sketched out a model of the endogenous development of a core-periphery economic geography, based on the interaction of economies of scale, transportation costs, and migration. As presented, however, the model had quite a few loose ends—that is, it wasn't really a fully specified model. The purpose of this appendix is to lay out a version of the same story that does not have any loose ends: a fully specified, general equilibrium core-periphery model. As we will see, the same basic conclusions emerge.[1]

Assumptions of the Model

We consider a country that contains two locations, East and West, and produces two kinds of goods, agricultural and manufactured. Agricultural production is homogeneous, produced under constant returns and perfect competition. Manu-

---

1. Actually, this formal model came first (Krugman 1991a). The informal version presented in lecture 1 was initially devised as a way to present some intuition about why this formal model works the way it does; I think of it as the "lite" version (less rigor, same taste).

factures consists of a number of differentiated products, each produced subject to economies of scale, with a monopolistically competitive market structure.

Everyone in the economy is assumed to share the same tastes. Welfare is a Cobb-Douglas function of consumption of agricultural goods and a manufactures aggregate:

$$U = C_M^{\pi} C_A^{(1-\pi)}. \tag{A.1}$$

Note that given this functional form, π is the share of expenditures that falls on manufactures.

The manufactures aggregate is in turn a CES function of consumption of individual manufactured goods, of which there is a large number, not all of them actually produced:

$$C_M = \left[\sum_i c_i^{\frac{\sigma-1}{\sigma}} \right]^{\frac{\sigma}{\sigma-1}}. \tag{A.2}$$

As long as a large number of manufactured goods are produced, this functional form ensures that the elasticity of demand for any individual good is simply σ.

There are two factors of production, each of which is specific to a particular sector. "Farmers" produce agricultural goods, "workers" produce manufactured goods; farmers cannot become workers or vice versa. To save notation we choose units so that there are a total of $1-\pi$ farmers and π workers (this choice of units leads to the result that the wages of farmers and workers are equal in equilibrium).

The geographical distribution of farmers is taken as fixed, with $(1-\pi)/2$ farmers in each location. Workers move to whichever location offers them a higher real income.

Farmers produce their goods under constant returns to scale. The economies of scale in manufacturing take the form of a linear cost function, in which a fixed cost in terms of manufacturing labor must be incurred in order to produce any individual variety of manufactures:

$$L_{Mi} = \alpha + \beta\, x_{Mi}. \tag{A.3}$$

Finally, we assume that there are costs of transporting manufactured goods between the two locations. These take Samuelson's "iceberg" form, in which only a fraction of a good that is shipped arrives (so that in effect transport costs are incurred in the good shipped). We let $\tau < 1$ be the fraction of a manufactured good shipped that actually arrives. Transportation of agricultural goods is assumed to be costless, an assumption made for analytical convenience; it ensures that the wage rate of farmers and the price of agricultural goods is the same in the two locations.

Pricing and Competition

Because there are a large number of potential manufactured goods, each of them produced subject to economies of scale, there is no reason for any two firms to try to produce the same good; the market structure of manufactures will therefore be one of monopolistic competition.

The producer of any one good will face an elasticity of demand σ. Her profit-maximizing price is therefore a constant markup over marginal cost,

$$p_i = \frac{\sigma}{\sigma-1} \beta w, \tag{A.4}$$

where w is the wage rate of manufacturing workers.

If there is free entry, however, profits will be driven to zero. The zero-profit condition may be written

$$(p - \beta w)x = \alpha w. \tag{A.5}$$

Note that with zero profits, price equals average cost. But this means that the ratio of average cost to marginal cost—which is one measure of economies of scale—is simply $\sigma/(\sigma-1)$. Thus equilibrium economies of scale are a function only of σ, so that σ, even though it is a parameter of tastes rather than technology, nonetheless acts as a sort of inverse index of the importance of increasing returns.

The zero-profit and pricing conditions together imply that the output of a representative manufacturing firm is

$$x = \frac{\alpha(\sigma - 1)}{\beta}.\qquad\qquad\text{(A.6)}$$

Consider a region with a resident labor force of L_M workers; the number of manufactured goods that region will produce is

$$n = \frac{L_M}{\alpha + \beta x} = \frac{L_M}{\alpha\sigma}.\qquad\qquad\text{(A.7)}$$

Sustainability of a Core-Periphery Pattern

We now ask the following question: is a situation in which all manufacturing is concentrated in one location, leaving the other location with only agriculture, an equilibrium? It doesn't matter which location we choose; so we examine the sustainability of an equilibrium with East as the manufacturing core and West as the agricultural periphery.

As we will see in a moment, there are two "centripetal" forces tending to keep a manufacturing core in existence, and one "centrifugal" force tending to pull it apart. Holding the core together are (1) the desire of firms to locate close to the larger market, and (2) the desire of workers to have access to the goods produced by other workers. These two forces may be thought of as corresponding respectively to the backward and forward linkage concepts of Hirschman (1958). Tending to break the core apart is the incentive of firms to move out to serve the peripheral agricultural market. What we will do is derive a criterion that determines whether the backward and forward linkages are strong enough to sustain an established core.

We begin by noting that given our choice of units, the wage rates of workers and farmers will be equal. That is, a share of expenditure π is spent on manufactured goods (including those goods that "melt" in transit), and (since profits are zero) ends up as wages of workers; but we have also chosen units so that a fraction π of the population are workers. So given this choice of unit the wage rates will necessarily be equal.

Now ask how the incomes of the two regions compare. East has half of the farmers, who receive a share $(1-\pi)/2$ of total income, plus all of the workers, receiving a share π. Let total income be unity; then the income of East is

$$Y^E = \frac{1+\pi}{2}. \tag{A.8}$$

West, on the other hand, has only its immobile farmers, who receive a share $(1-\pi)/2$ of income; so the income of West is

$$Y^W = \frac{1-\pi}{2}. \tag{A.9}$$

This situation, in which all manufacturing is concentrated in East, will be sustainable if it is unprofitable for any firms to enter in West. So we must determine if it is profitable for an individual firm to "defect" by commencing production in West.

Let n be the (large) number of firms currently producing in East. Then the sales of each of these firms will be

$$s^E = \frac{\pi}{n}.$$ (A.10)

If a firm were to try to start production in West, it would need to attract workers. To do this, it would need to pay a higher wage than Eastern firms are paying, since all manufactured goods (except for its own negligible contribution) would have to be imported. Recall that only a fraction τ of a good that is shipped arrives. The price of manufactured goods in West will therefore be $1/\tau$ times as high as that in East. The overall price index, which is a geometric average of manufactures and agricultural goods, will thus be $\tau^{-\pi}$ times as high. In order to attract workers, a defecting firm must match the real wage of established firms and thus pay a nominal wage that is $\tau^{-\pi}$ times that paid in East.

But the price charged by a firm is a fixed markup on its marginal cost, which in turn is proportional to wages. So the price charged by a new Western firm will exceed that of established Eastern firms in the ratio

$$p^W = p^E \tau^{-\pi}.$$ (A.11)

The prices to consumers may differ from the prices charged by firms because of transport costs. For a consumer in East, the relative price of a Western good is higher than the price in (A.11), by the fraction $1/\tau$; that is, the relative consumer price is $p_W/\tau p_E$. For a consumer in West, it is the Eastern good that incurs shipping costs; for her, the relative price of the Western good is $\tau p_W/p_E$.

A 1 percent increase in the relative price of the Western good reduces the consumption of that good relative to the consumption of a representative Eastern product by σ percent. Because of the higher price, however, the higher price reduces relative *expenditure* by only $\sigma - 1$ percent. We can use this result to derive the value of the sales of a defecting firm. Bearing in mind the incomes of East and West, it is

$$s^W = \frac{\pi}{n}\left[\frac{1+\pi}{2}\left(\frac{p^W}{p^E \tau}\right)^{-(\sigma-1)} + \frac{1-\pi}{2}\left(\frac{p^W \tau}{p^E}\right)^{-(\sigma-1)}\right]. \tag{A.12}$$

Let us express these sales relative to those of a typical established Eastern firm; dividing by equation (A.10), we have

$$\frac{s^W}{s^E} = \frac{1+\pi}{2}\tau^{(1+\pi)(\sigma-1)} + \frac{1-\pi}{2}\tau^{-(1-\pi)(\sigma-1)}. \tag{A.13}$$

Now firms will charge a constant markup over marginal costs. Thus they earn an operating surplus that is a constant fraction of sales. It thus may at first seem that it will be profitable to defect if and only if $s_W/s_E > 1$. But this is not quite right, because the fixed cost that must be covered by operating profits is also incurred in labor, and is therefore also higher for a defecting firm in the ratio τ^π. It is only profitable to defect if

$$s_W/s_E > \tau^{-\pi}. \tag{A.14}$$

So we define a new variable, K, equal to $\tau^{-\pi}s_W/s_E$:

$$K = \frac{\tau^{\pi\sigma}}{2}\left[(1+\pi)\,\tau^{\sigma-1} + (1-\pi)\,\tau^{-(\sigma-1)}\right].$$ (A.15)

If K is greater than one, it will be profitable to start production in West; only if $K < 1$ is a core-periphery equilibrium sustainable.

As we see, K is an index that depends on the three parameters of the model: π, the share of manufactures in expenditure; τ, which is an inverse measure of transportation costs; and σ, which is inversely related to equilibrium economies of scale. The next step is to clarify the nature of that dependence.

Determinants of the Nature of Equilibrium

What K does is to define a boundary: a set of values for which a core-periphery pattern is just sustainable. To trace this boundary we need to evaluate the properties of K around 1: if one of the parameters is changed in that neighborhood, how must either of the others change to leave K unchanged?

The easiest parameter to evaluate is the share of manufactures in expenditure, π. We find that

$$\frac{\partial K}{\partial \pi} = \sigma K \ln(\tau) + \tau^{\sigma\pi}\left[\tau^{\sigma-1} - \tau^{-(\sigma-1)}\right] < 0.$$ (A.16)

The effect of an increased π on K is unambiguously negative—that is, a higher share of manufacturing in income makes a core-periphery pattern more likely. There are two reasons, represented by the two terms in (A.16). First, the size of the wage premium that must be paid by a defecting firm, which gives rise to a forward linkage, becomes stronger. Second, the relative size of the core market, which gives rise to a backward linkage, also becomes stronger.

Consider next the effect of transportation costs. By inspecting (A.15), we can see the following. First, when $\tau = 1$, $K = 1$: when transportation costs are zero, location is irrelevant. Second, when τ is very small (transportation costs very high), K approaches

$$\lim K_{\tau \to 0} = \frac{1}{2} \tau^{1- \sigma (1- \pi)} . \tag{A.17}$$

Unless σ is small (economies of scale large) or π large, this becomes arbitrarily large for low τ. Let us provisionally assume that $\sigma(1 - \pi) > 1$; the economics of the alternative case will become apparent shortly.

Finally, we differentiate (A.15) with respect to τ:

$$\frac{\partial K}{\partial \tau} = \frac{\sigma \tau K}{\tau} + (\sigma -1)\frac{\tau^{\sigma \pi}}{2}\left[(1 + \pi)\tau^{\sigma -2} - (1-\pi)\tau^{-\sigma}\right] . \tag{A.18}$$

Although the sign of (A.18) is in general ambiguous, the second term and hence the whole expression are always positive for τ close to 1.

Putting these observations together, we get a shape for K as a function of τ that looks like figure A.1. K is greater than one for small values of τ, falls below one at some critical level of transport costs, then approaches one from below. Only in the upper range of τ, with relatively low transport cost, is a core-periphery pattern sustainable. Note also that in the vicinity of the critical value of τ, the derivative of K with respect to τ is negative.

The case where $\sigma(1 - \pi) < 1$ can also now be interpreted. This is a situation where economies of scale are so strong, and the share of manufactures so large, that workers will have a higher real wage in the location with a larger manufacturing sector even if transportation costs are infinite.

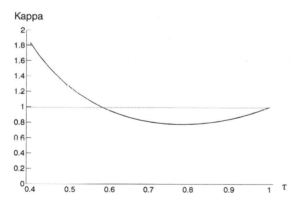

Figure A.1

Finally, we turn to the effect of σ. We find that

$$\frac{\partial K}{\partial \sigma} = \pi K \ln(\tau) + \frac{\tau^{\pi\sigma}}{2}(\sigma-1)\ln(\tau)\left[(1+\pi)\tau^{\sigma-1}-(1-\pi)\tau^{-(\sigma-1)}\right]. \quad \text{(A.19)}$$

By comparing (A.19) with (A.18), we see that if the derivative of K with respect to τ is negative, as it must be near the boundary, the derivative with respect to σ must be positive.

Now we can investigate the shape of the boundary. First hold σ constant, and plot the critical value of τ as a function of π. We know that

$$\frac{\partial \tau}{\partial \pi} = -\frac{\partial K / \partial \pi}{\partial K / \partial \tau} < 0 \, . \quad\quad\quad\quad\quad\quad \text{(A.20)}$$

Thus the boundary in π, τ space is downward sloping, as shown in figure A.2. Given our earlier discussion, it must intersect the vertical axis at $\tau = 1$, and the horizontal axis at $\pi = (\sigma - 1)/\sigma$.

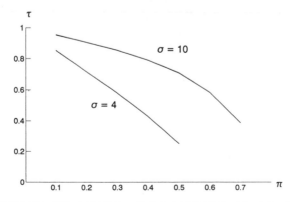

Figure A.2

This boundary will be shifted out if σ is increased. We know that

$$\frac{\partial \pi}{\partial \sigma} = -\frac{\partial K / \partial \sigma}{\partial K / \partial \pi} > 0 .$$

(A.21)

So an increase in σ, which represents a *decrease* in the importance of scale economies, shifts the boundary to the right, making it harder to sustain a core-periphery pattern.

We see, then, that this formal model essentially confirms the story told more loosely in lecture 1. A pattern in which one location emerges as the manufacturing core, while the other becomes an agricultural periphery, depends on some combination of large economies of scale, low transportation costs, and a large share of manufacturing in expenditure.

Appendix B:

History versus Expectations

In the discussion of the process of change in the first lecture, the issue of expectations inevitably arose. Suppose that the external economies arising from the interaction of scale economies and transportation costs are in fact large enough to generate a core-periphery pattern. Which region will emerge as the core? It is natural to suppose that the region that gets a head start in industrialization will become the core, but a little thought shows that this is not necessarily true. For if everyone for some reason comes to believe that another region will become the core, and then acts on that belief by moving there, this will be a self-fulfilling prophecy.

So we need to worry about the relative importance of "history," that is, initial conditions, as opposed to "expectations," that is, self-fulfilling prophecy, in determining the location of core and periphery.

In this appendix I offer a suggestive approach, based on Krugman 1991b. Ideally, this analysis would be based on an explicit dynamization of the formal core-periphery model set out in appendix A. In practice, that is too difficult; to make the problem tractable, it is necessary to assume a linearity that is strictly speaking inconsistent with that model. The basic spirit of the model is, however, preserved, and one can hope that this approach still yields useful insights.

Consider, then, an economy that consists of two regions. There is one factor of production, workers, that can move between the regions. Instead of explicitly modeling the external economies, we simply assume that the difference between real wage rates in region 1 and region 2 is increasing in the share of the total labor force L that is located in region 1:

$$w_1 - w_2 = \alpha \left(L_1 - \overline{L_1} \right).$$

(B.1)

The natural ad hoc assumption to make is that labor migrates toward the region that offers the higher real wage rate; and that simple assumption is in fact the one made in the discussion and diagrams in lecture 1. For current purposes, however, we assume more sophisticated behavior on the part of potential migrants. First, we assume that there is a cost to moving, which is convex in the aggregate rate of movement. Thus the total income of workers is equal to their wages less a deduction for these moving costs, which we assume to be quadratic:

$$Y = w_1 L_1 + w_2 L_2 - \frac{1}{2\gamma} \left(\dot{L_1} \right)^2.$$

(B.2)

Next, we assume that workers are forward-looking. Indeed, they have perfect foresight about the future path of real wages in the two regions. This allows them to put a present value on the state of being in one region as opposed to the other. Let r be the discount rate (I do not try here to go the whole way to a model in which this discount rate itself is endogenous). Then at any time t the value of being in region 1 instead of region 2—a kind of asset, albeit one that could take on a negative value—is

$$q(t) = \int_t^\infty \left[w_1(\tau) - w_2(\tau) \right] e^{-r(\tau-t)} d\tau .$$
(B.3)

We can now turn to the dynamics of migration. The rate at which workers move will be such that the marginal cost of moving to region 1 is equal to the gain in shifting location. This implies that

$$\dot{L}_1 = \gamma q .$$
(B.4)

By differentiating (B.3) (or by thinking of standard asset pricing), we have

$$\dot{q} = rq - (w_1 - w_2)$$
$$= rq - \alpha(L_1 - \overline{L}) .$$
(B.5)

Equations (B.4) and (B.5) define a dynamic system in q and L_1. The laws of motion of that system are illustrated in figure B.1. Clearly the central equilibrium is unstable; the system must converge over time either to point 1, where the whole labor force is concentrated in region 1, or to point 2, where the labor

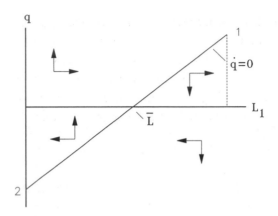

Figure B.1

force is concentrated in region 2. Given an initial allocation of the labor force, the "asset price" q will jump to a level that puts the economy on a path leading to one equilibrium or the other; such a path will, by construction, be an equilibrium in the sense that expectations of economic agents are in fact validated. But what path does the economy follow, and which region does it converge to?

The pair of differential equations (B.4) and (B.5) have two roots; they are

$$\lambda_1 = \frac{r + \sqrt{r^2 - 4\alpha\gamma}}{2}$$

$$\lambda_2 = \frac{r - \sqrt{r^2 - 4\alpha\gamma}}{2}. \qquad (B.6)$$

Either both roots are positive, or both are complex. These define two qualitative cases.

If both roots are positive, then the path followed by the economy can have at most one reversal of direction. Thus the only paths leading to long-run equilibrium that are consistent with the laws of motion illustrated in figure B.1 are those shown in figure B.2.

The economic interpretation of figure B.2 is that the labor force eventually concentrates in whatever region started out with more workers. The only role of expectations here is to reinforce the role of history. Suppose that region 1 starts out with more workers; then workers considering moving will realize that it will attract still more workers, and strengthen its advantage over region 2. They therefore will assign a greater value to being in region 1, and hence move more rapidly, than the

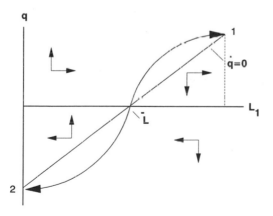

Figure B.2

present value of the current wage differential. This is reflected in the fact that the S-shaped curve shown in the figure is steeper than the line of equal real wages.

What if the roots are complex? Both will have positive real parts; so any path will spiral outward from the singularity in the middle. In the long run L_1 will reach either 0 or the total labor force L, and q will be the present discounted value of the wage differential at that labor force allocation. So the possible paths are, as shown in figure B.3, the two spiral arms that lead outward from the center to the two possible long-run equilibria.

What does this artistically remarkable figure tell us? One should not focus on the spirals too much, for reasons that will be clear in a moment. The important point, instead, is that there is a range of inital values of L_1 from which either long-run

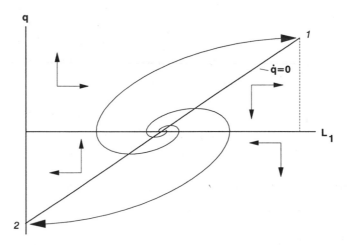

Figure B.3

equilibrium can be reached. If L_1 starts anywhere in the region of overlapping spirals, then there exists at least one path of self-fulfilling expectations leading to either long-run equilibrium. In other words, we can start with, say, 60 percent of manufacturing in region 1, but with everyone expecting region 2 to emerge as the core—and the rational actions of individuals based on that belief will in fact confirm that expectation.

Let us refer to the range of labor allocations from which either long-run equilibrium can be reached as the "overlap." Evidently, if an overlap exists and L_1 lies within it, the model is subject to a basic indeterminacy. In fact, the indeterminacy is even worse than may at first appear. As we see in figure B.3, given an initial value of L_1 within the overlap, there may be several paths leading in each direction. Furthermore, there is no reason to restrict oneself to deterministic paths. One could instead have stochastic paths, in which workers assign some probability to discrete jumps in q that may lead to sudden reversals in the direction of labor migration; essentially, within the overlap we are in the sunspot-and-rational-bubble territory so beloved of monetary theorists.

Not much can be said, then, about what happens inside the overlap. But we can still ask how likely these strange possibilities are. When is there an overlap, and how large is it?

The existence of an overlap depends on the roots (B.6) being complex. This then gives us our criterion for an overlap:

$$r^2 < 4\alpha\gamma \, . \tag{B.7}$$

This has a clear economic interpretation. First, an overlap is more likely to happen if the discount rate is low, so that people weight the future wage differential (which depends on what they expect each other to do) heavily relative to the present. Second, an overlap will occur if the external economies that make people want to do the same thing as everyone else are high. Finally, and most importantly, an overlap will exist if the rate at which resources can be reallocated between regions is high, so that expectations can be self-fulfilling.

The same factors that determine whether an overlap will exist determine its extent—that is, the range of initial conditions for which there exist self-fulfilling expectations that lead to convergence in either direction. In particular, as the speed of adjustment increases, the overlap grows, eventually encompassing the whole space.

What does this model have to say about reality? My guess is that for core-periphery issues at a grand level, history rules, and expectations at best help it along. The pace at which capital and labor can shift between regions is simply too slow to imagine otherwise: I do not believe that it is realistic to imagine that events at the level of, say, the rise of the sunbelt can happen fast enough potentially to constitute self-fulfilling prophecies.

When it comes to smaller-scale events, however, I am not so sure. The rise and decline of individual cities, and perhaps of somewhat larger regions, may indeed sometimes be the result of self-fulfilling optimism and pessimism.

Appendix C:

Labor Market Pooling

In lecture 2 I attempted to suggest why pooling of a market for specialized labor is beneficial, using two-firm examples and focusing on the case of predetermined wages. In this appendix I try to suggest the wider reach of the general idea by offering a slightly different model, in which we allow a larger number of firms and assume that the labor market always clears.

Suppose, then, that there are a number of firms. We represent each firm by a revenue function in which labor is the only argument, and for the sake of the example suppose that the function is quadratic, with additive firm-specific shocks to the marginal revenue product of labor:

$$R_i = \alpha + (\beta + \varepsilon_i) L_i - \frac{\gamma}{2} L_i^2. \tag{C.1}$$

We ignore the possibility that firms will act as oligopsonists in the labor market. Each firm will simply set the marginal revenue product of labor equal to the wage rate:

$$w = \beta + \varepsilon_i - \gamma L_i. \tag{C.2}$$

This implies a labor demand function from each firm:

$$L_i = \frac{\beta + \varepsilon_i - w}{\gamma}. \tag{C.3}$$

Within the location, we assume that the labor market clears:

$$\sum_{i=1}^{n} L_i = L, \tag{C.4}$$

where n is the number of firms.

The wage rate will depend on the number of workers, the number of firms, and on the shocks experienced by the individual firms:

$$w = \beta - \frac{\gamma L}{n} + \frac{1}{n} \sum_i \varepsilon_i. \tag{C.5}$$

Let us now assume that the shocks experienced by the firms are uncorrelated, with a variance σ^2. Then we may show, first, that the expected wage rate depends only on the ratio of the labor force to the number of firms:

$$Ew = \beta - \frac{\gamma L}{n}. \tag{C.6}$$

The variance of the expected wage depends on the number of firms:

$$\text{var}\ (w) = \frac{\sigma^2}{n}. \tag{C.7}$$

The covariance of the wage with firm-specific shocks also depends on the number of firms:

$$\text{cov}\ (w, \varepsilon_1) = \frac{\sigma^2}{n}. \tag{C.8}$$

The profits of a firm are its revenue less its wage costs:

$$\pi_i = R_i - wL_i. \tag{C.9}$$

From C.1, C.5, and C.9, it is possible to solve for the profits of a firm as a function of L, n, and the firm-specific shocks; it is then possible, after tedious substitution, to arrive at the surprisingly simple expression for *expected* profits,

$$E\pi = \alpha + \frac{1}{\gamma}\left(\frac{L}{n}\right)^2 + \frac{1}{2}\frac{n-1}{n}\sigma^2. \tag{C.10}$$

We now have expressions for expected wages and expected profits as a function of the number of firms and workers in a given location.

Suppose, now, that there are two locations, 1 and 2, with both firms and workers free to choose in which location to settle. The total number of firms is n; of this, n_1 locate in 1, n_2 in 2. Similarly, of the L workers, L_1 locate in 1, L_2 in 2. What are the possible equilibrium configurations?

One equilibrium, of course, is an even split of both firms and workers. This is shown in figure C.1 by the point labeled 1. This is, however, an unstable equilibrium.

To see why, we draw in the loci for which firms and workers respectively are indifferent between the two locations. For workers this is straightforward: expected wages depend only on the ratio of firms to workers, so that the locus of worker indifference WW corresponds to a line with slope L/n.

For firms, we first note that the difference between the profits of a firm in location 1 and one in location 2 is

$$\pi_1 - \pi_2 = \frac{1}{\gamma}\left[\left(\frac{L_1}{n_1}\right)^2 - \left(\frac{L_2}{n_2}\right)^2\right] + \frac{1}{2}\sigma^2\left[\frac{n_1-1}{n_1} - \frac{n_2-1}{n_2}\right]. \tag{C.11}$$

In the vicinity of $n_1 = n_2$, $L_1 = L_2$, the effects of reallocating firms and workers to location 1 are

West's share
of firms

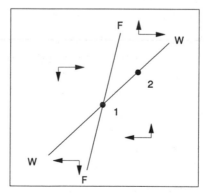

West's share
of workers

Figure C. 1

$$\frac{d(\pi_1 - \pi_2)}{dL_1} = \frac{4}{\gamma} \frac{L}{n^2} > 0 . \tag{C.12}$$

and

$$\frac{d(\pi_1 - \pi_2)}{dn_1} = -\frac{4}{\gamma} \frac{L^2}{n^3} - 1\sigma^2 \frac{1}{n_1^2} < 0 . \tag{C.13}$$

It is immediately apparent that the locus $\pi_1 = \pi_2$, FF in the figure, is upward sloping. It is also easy to demonstrate that it is steeper than WW, either directly from equations (C.12) and (C.13) or (what I find more useful) by a graphical argument. Consider point 2 in figure C.1. At that point the *ratio* of firms to workers is the same in both locations, but location 1 has more of both. From (C.10) it is therefore apparent that firms are more profitable in location 1. So FF must lie above WW at that point.

We are now home free. Assume that workers move toward the location that offers higher expected wages and that firms move toward the location that offers higher expected profits. The dynamics of the model are then indicated by the arrows. Point 1 is unstable; the system is driven to a corner, with all firms and workers concentrated in one location or the other.

Appendix D:

Locational Gini Coefficients

The following tables present "locational Gini coefficients" for U.S. three-digit industries; the concept and method of calculation is explained in the text. The table contains the following information:

1. The industry rank by Gini.
2. The industry code.
3. The industry description.
4. The Gini.
5. The three leading states in employment within the industry.

Rank	SIC	Description	Gini	Main states
1.	303	Reclaimed rubber	0.5	WY,WI,WV
2.	313	Boot and shoe cut stock & findings	0.482845	ME,MO,MA
3.	315	Leather gloves and mittens	0.48233	WI,NY,WY
4.	222	Weaving mills, synthetics	0.476676	GA,SC,NC
5.	237	Fur goods	0.468169	NY,WY,WI
6.	223	Weaving and finishing mills, wool	0.451512	ME,RI,NH
7.	221	Weaving mills, cotton	0.443084	SC,GA,NC
8.	319	Leather goods, nec	0.442542	TX,MA,CA
9.	227	Floor covering mills	0.432963	GA,SC,VA
10.	228	Yarn and thread mills	0.428421	NC,GA,SC
11.	386	Photographic equip. & supplies	0.428276	CO,MN,OK

12.	277	Greeting card publishing	0.427133	AR,KS,MO
13.	224	Narrow fabric mills	0.423601	RI,NH,NC
14.	385	Ophthalmic goods	0.414319	AZ,RI,MA
15.	376	Guided missiles, space veh., parts	0.411017	CA,UT,AZ
16.	374	Railroad equip.	0.410767	PA,IL,WV
17.	226	Textile finishing, except wool	0.410014	SC,NC,RI
18.	304	Rubber and plastics hose & belting	0.408587	NE,CO,OH
19.	235	Hats, caps, and millinery	0.407575	IA,MO,NY
20.	316	Luggage	0.404685	RI,CO,TN
21.	302	Rubber and plastics footwear	0.402163	ME,NH,MD
22.	396	Costume jewelry and notions	0.400823	RI,CT,NE
23.	391	Jewelry, silverware, & plated ware	0.397361	RI,UT,NM
24.	375	Motorcycles, bicycles, & parts	0.396409	NE,TN,OK
25.	387	Watches, clocks, & watchcases	0.388946	AR,CT,MS
26.	311	Leather and leather products	0.387232	ME,NH,WI
27.	317	Handbags & other per leather gds	0.379857	NY,RI,MA
28.	333	Primary nonferrous metals	0.366064	MT,NM,WA
29.	225	Knitting mills	0.365623	NC,TN,VA
30.	373	Ship & boat bldg & repairing	0.363088	MS,FL,ME
31.	372	Aircraft and parts	0.352313	KS,CT,NV
32.	393	Musical instruments	0.345101	MS,AR,IN
33.	253	Public bldg & related furniture	0.344445	AR,CT,MS
34.	379	Misc. transportation equipment	0.326485	IN,NB,MI
35.	352	Farm and garden machinery	0.324905	ND,IA,NE
36.	272	Periodicals	0.324702	DC,NY,IL
37.	287	Agricultural chemicals	0.324638	ID,LA,FL
38.	383	Optical instruments & lenses	0.323826	NH,MA,CT
39.	301	Tires and inner tubes	0.320952	OK,AL,IA
40.	365	Radio & tv receiving equipment	0.320622	TN,AR,MO
41.	282	Plastics materials & synthetics	0.319335	DE,SC,VA
42.	348	Ordinance & accessories, nec	0.316472	VT,NV,MN
43.	334	Secondary nonferrous metals	0.310073	SC,AL,IN
44.	286	Industrial organic chemicals	0.309039	WV,LA,TX
45.	314	Footwear, except rubber	0.308738	ME,NH,MO
46.	351	Engines and turbines	0.305607	WI,MD,MI
47.	331	Blast furnace & basic steel pdts	0.303562	WV,IN,PA
48.	229	Miscellaneous textile goods	0.303407	RI,SC,ME
49.	371	Motor vehicles & equipment	0.302518	MI,OH,DE
50.	395	Pens,pencils,& office & art supplies	0.30166	RI,IA,NJ
51.	236	Childrens outerwear	0.296566	SC,ME,RI
52.	339	Misc primary metal products	0.293852	MI,CT,IN
53.	234	Womens & childrens undergarments	0.292174	AL,MS,GA

54.	232	Mens & boys furnishings	0.289464	MS,AL,GA
55.	357	Office & computing machines	0.283499	MN,AZ,CO
56.	231	Mens & boys suits & coats	0.281515	PA,MD,GA
57.	281	Industrial inorganic chemicals	0.278271	HI,TN,NV
58.	363	Household appliances	0.27411	SD,TN,IA
59.	381	Eng & scientific instruments	0.266791	DE,AZ,WA
60.	238	Misc apparel & accessories	0.259691	MD,MS,NY
61.	251	Household furniture	0.255488	NS,MS,VA
62.	259	Misc furniture & fixtures	0.255273	UT,RI,MD
63.	346	Metal forgings & stampings	0.254278	MI,OH,WI
64.	353	Construction & related machinery	0.25105	OK,WY,IA
65.	274	Miscellaneous publishing	0.244823	DC,CO,KS
66.	345	Screw machine pdts, bolts, etc	0.239701	RI,CT,IL
67.	271	Newspapers	0.237544	NY,VT,MN
68.	273	Books	0.237544	NY,VT,MN
69.	279	Printing trade services	0.235163	DC,MD,NY
70.	283	Drugs	0.234789	NJ,IN,DE
71.	278	Blankbooks & bookbinding	0.232561	MA,NJ,MO
72.	341	Metal cans & shipping containers	0.232013	CO,MD,IL
73.	233	Womens & misses outerwear	0.231918	HI,NY,PA
74.	354	Metalworking machinery	0.231087	VT,MI,OH
75.	252	Office furniture	0.230208	MI,IA,NC
76.	382	Measuring and controlling devices	0.224846	NV,VT,NH
77.	366	Communication equipment	0.224418	MD,NM,FL
78.	332	Iron & steel foundries	0.22053	AL,WI,OH
79.	306	Fabricated rubber pdts, nec	0.217496	OH,NH,AR
80.	367	Electronic components & accessories	0.216259	AZ,VT,CA
81.	336	Nonferrous foundries	0.215594	OH,MI,WI
82.	284	Soaps, cleaners & toilet goods	0.210857	NJ,MO,MD
83.	343	Plumbing & heating, except electric	0.201985	VT,WV,KY
84.	285	Paints & allied products	0.201037	NY,IL,KY
85.	361	Electric distributing equipment	0.197298	MS,KY,PA
86.	335	Nonferrous rolling & drawing	0.194648	WV,RI,NV
87.	364	Elec lighting & wiring equip	0.186535	RI,WV,IL
88.	254	Partitions & fixtures	0.182132	NE,AR,IL
89.	239	Misc fabricated textile pdt	0.180902	ND,HI,SC
90.	362	Electrical industrial apparatus	0.180583	WI,AR,OH
91.	347	Metal services, nec	0.180022	RI,MI,CA
92.	342	Cutlery, hand tools, & hardware	0.17853	CT,MI,WV
93.	289	Miscellaneous chemical products	0.173693	NM,KS,NJ
94.	384	Medical instruments & supplies	0.170018	SD,UT,NE
95.	358	Refrigeration & service machinery	0.163089	KY,MN,TN
96.	394	Toys & sporting goods	0.160812	RI,NJ,VT

97.	276	Mainfold business forms	0.155267	VT,UT,KS
98.	356	General industrial machinery	0.153676	OK,NH,CT
99.	355	Special industry machinery	0.148829	NH,MA,WI
100.	349	Misc fabricated metal products	0.140874	OK,RI,IA
101.	369	Misc electrical equipment & sup	0.137169	VT,IN,CO
102.	399	Miscellaneous manufactures	0.128871	NV,IL,NY
103.	344	Fabricated structural metal pdts	0.119871	OK,LA,RI
104.	359	Misc machinery, except electrical	0.109036	NM,OK,LA
105.	275	Commercial printing	0.101342	DC,MN,IL
106.	307	Misc plastics products	0.096105	NV,NH,NJ

References

Arthur, B. (1986). "Industry location patterns and the importance of history," Center for Economic Policy Research (Stanford), paper #84.

Arthur, B. (1990). "Positive feedbacks in the economy," *Scientific American* 262 (February): 92–99.

Bairoch, P. (1988). *Cities and Economic Development*, Chicago: University of Chicago Press.

Buckberg, E. (1990). "Settling the prairies: Canada's national policy in the late 19th century," mimeo, MIT.

Chandler, A. (1990). *Scale and Scope*, Cambridge, MA: Harvard University Press.

David, P. (1985). "Clio and the economics of QWERTY," *American Economic Review* 75: 332–337.

David, P., and Rosenbloom, J. (1990). "Marshallian factor market externalities and the dynamics of industrial localization," *Journal of Urban Economics*.

DeGeer, S. (1927). "The American manufacturing belt," *Geografiska Annaler* 9: 233–359.

Dixit, A., and Stiglitz, J. (1977). "Monopolistic competition and optimum product diversity," *American Economic Review*.

Faini, R. (1984). "Increasing returns, nontraded inputs, and regional developments," *Economic Journal* 94: 308–323.

Hall, R. (1989). "Temporal agglomeration," NBER Working Paper # 3143.

Helpman, E., and Krugman, P. (1985). *Market Structure and Foreign Trade*, Cambridge, MA: MIT Press.

Henderson, J. V. (1974). "The sizes and types of cities," *American Economic Review* 64: 640–656.

Henderson, J. V. (1988). *Urban Development: Theory, Fact, and Illusion*, New York: Oxford.

Hirschman, A. (1958). *The Strategy of Economic Development*, New Haven: Yale University Press.

Hoover, E. M. (1948). *The Location of Economic Activity*, New York: McGraw-Hill.

Isard, W. (1956). *Location and Space-economy*, Cambridge, MA: MIT Press.

Jacobs, J. (1969). *The Economy of Cities*, New York: Vintage Books.

Jacobs, J. (1984). *Cities and the Wealth of Nations*, New York: Vintage Books.

Kaldor, N. (1972). "The irrelevance of equilibrium economics," *Economic Journal* 82: 1237–1255.

Krugman, P. (1981). "Trade, accumulation, and uneven development," *Journal of Development Economics* 8: 149–161.

Krugman, P. (1991a). "History and industry location: the case of the US manufacturing belt," *American Economic Review*.

Krugman, P. (1991b). "Increasing returns and economic geography," *Journal of Political Economy*, forthcoming.

Krugman, P. (1991c). "History vs. Expectations," *Quarterly Journal of Economics*, forthcoming.

Krugman, P., and Venables, A. (1990). "Integation and the competitiveness of peripheral industry," in C. Bliss and J. Braga de Macedo, eds., *Unity with Diversity in the European Community*, Cambridge: Cambridge University Press.

Lichtenberg, R. M. (1960). *One Tenth of a Nation*, Cambridge, MA: Harvard University Press.

Marshall, A. (1920). *Principles of Economics*, London: Macmillan.

McCarty, H. H. (1940). *The Geographic Basis of American Life*, Westport, CT: Greenwood Press.

Murphy, K., Shleifer, A., and Vishny, R. (1989a). "Industrialization and the big push," *Journal of Political Economy* 97: 1003–1026.

Murphy, K., Shleifer, A., and Vishny, R. (1989b). "Increasing returns, durables, and economic fluctuations," NBER Working Paper #3014.

Myers, D. (1983), "Emergence of the American manufacturing belt: an interpretation," *Journal of Historical Geography* 9: 145–174.

Myrdal, G. (1957). *Economic Theory and Underdeveloped Regions*, London: Duckworth.

Perloff, H., Dunn, E., Lampard, E., and Muth, R. (1960). *Regions, Resources, and Economic Growth*, Baltimore: Johns Hopkins.

Porter, M. (1990). *The Competitive Advantage of Nations*, New York: Free Press.

Pred, A. (1966). *The Spatial Dynamics of US Urban-Industrial Growth, 1800–1914*, Cambridge, MA: MIT Press.

Rhode, P. (1988). "Growth in a high-wage economy: California, 1890–1920," mimeo, Stanford.

Romer, P. (1986). "Increasing returns and long-run growth," *Journal of Political Economy* 94, 1002–1038.

Romer, P. (1987). "Growth based on increasing returns due to specialization," *American Economic Review* 77: 56–62.

Romer, P. (1990). "Are nonconvexities important for understanding growth?," NBER Working Paper # 3271.

Rotemberg, J., and Saloner, G. (1990). "Competition and human capital accumulation: a theory of interregional specialization and trade," NBER Working Paper # 3228.

Young, A. (1928). "Increasing returns and economic progress," *Economic Journal* 38: 527–542.

Index